ONCE Upon a
RHYME
The East
Edited by Jenni Bannister

First published in Great Britain in 2011 by:
YoungWriters
Remus House
Coltsfoot Drive
Peterborough
PE2 9BF
Telephone: 01733 890066
Website: www.youngwriters.co.uk

Book Design by Tim Christian

SB ISBN 978-0-85739-499-6

THIS BOOK BELONGS TO

....

Foreword

Here at Young Writers our objective is to help children discover the joys of poetry and creative writing. Few things are more encouraging for the aspiring writer than seeing their own work in print. We are proud that our anthologies are able to give young authors this unique sense of confidence and pride in their abilities.

Once Upon a Rhyme is our latest fantastic competition, specifically designed to encourage the writing skills of primary school children through the medium of poetry. From the high quality of entries received, it is clear that Once Upon a Rhyme really captured the imagination of all involved.

The resulting collection is an excellent showcase for the poetic talents of the younger generation and we are sure you will be charmed and inspired by it, both now and in the future.

Contents

Maddie Stewart is our featured poet this year.
She has written a nonsense workshop for you
and included some of her great poems.
You can find these at the end of your book

Great Abington Primary School, Great Abington

Guyhirn CE (VC) Primary School, Guyhirn

La Salette RC Primary School, Rainham

Loyola Preparatory School, Buckhurst HIl

Notley Green Primary School, Great Notley

Oaklands School, Loughton

St James' RC Primary School, Orpington

Snodland CE Primary School, Snodland

The Daiglen School, Buckhurst Hill

Wethersfield CE (VC) Primary School, Wethersfield

Woodford Green Primary School, Woodford Green

Woodville Primary School, South Woodham Ferrers

The Poems

Juicy Orange

I am juicy, juicy
I am sweet
But if you bite into me . . .
You might get juicy, juicy,
Sticky, sticky fingers.

Yazmine Thompson (7)
Bardfield Primary School, Basildon

The Snail

Snails are friendly but just one thing
They leave slimy slime everywhere they go
If you feel carefully you might feel some scaly scales
The snail is as slow as a person walking slow
The snail has got a lot of brown on it
It is slippery, slippery like ice
And eats leafy leaves all day long.

Dayna Burgess (9)
Bardfield Primary School, Basildon

Sharks

Sharks are mean
And sharks are lean
And have such jagged teeth

Some are mean, some are nice
Some are big, some are small
And some are dirty.

Alfie Burman (8)
Bardfield Primary School, Basildon

It's Love You're Talking About

As red as a rose.
As pretty as a heart.
As lovely as a flower on a summer's day.
As fluffy as a teddy bear.
As cute as a puppy.

Tazmin Hewitson (9)
Bardfield Primary School, Basildon

The Catherine Wheel

The Catherine wheel,
Hanging from the fence,
Waiting for my moment,
Not long from now,
I'm so excited.

Yes! Here comes the flame,
I'm ready to dance,
I'm ready to twirl,
Ow, that hurt,
It's not every day you get burnt.

Oh boy, oh boy,
It's my moment,
Dancing like a ballerina,
Spitting sparks like a gun,
A very dizzy job.

Until I die,
Frazzle up,
Go into my never-ending sleep,
Forever gone,
The Catherine wheel.

Nicole Broughton (10)
Barnehurst Junior School, Erith

The Life Of A Catherine Wheel

Here I am,
Out in the freezing cold,
On a smoky Bonfire Night,
Waiting to have my turn on firework night.

I am right at the back,
Tied to the post,
Waiting for my turn to blast-off,
I'm not as loud as the others,
But I'm very colourful.

I'm trying to shout out to the people,
Not to blast me!
Once I'm gone,
I'm gone,
But at the same time, I love it!

That feeling of spinning round and round,
Giving out bright beautiful colours,
I am the most famous firework
And I am proud.

I can see someone heading towards me down the garden path,
I am so nervous but excited at the same time!
It's nearly my turn to show everyone what I do!

I'm ready,
The flame is on me,
It's getting to my face,
Bang!
I'm spinning around and around and around on the post!

It's making me dizzy but it's such great fun!
Oh, the beautiful colours people can see!
I'm sure they're all looking at me!
I'm fizzling and cracking into the air.

I'm coming to an end now
And I'm slowing down,
My sparkles are fading away,
I've had the best time,
It's great fun being a Catherine wheel.

Bethany Bird (11)
Barnehurst Junior School, Erith

The Amazing Rocket!

Grabbed out the box, what a fright!
Ugly faces not to my delight,
Sweaty fingers all over my body,
Making me dance with a twitch!

Put on the stick with a last twirl,
Putting my happiest face on as well!
They're about to light me, hold on tight!
Because I'll be like a thundering volcano!

Here I go!
3, 2, 1, blast-off!
Wow, it's high up here,
Look at my beautiful colours!

Smiling for the camera,
Trying not to sneeze,
Sparks are burning me,
Then I slowly fade away in the dark.

Amy Barton (11)
Barnehurst Junior School, Erith

The Explosive Firework!

As I wait to be lit up
I think of all the lovely colours that I will jump,
I make the sky brighten,
Oh boy, I just want to lighten!

One more then I'm going to be done,
I'm like a rocket,
Being shot to the sun,
I hope the pets don't make a fuss,
Because when I'm in the sky,
I'm like a huge octopus.

Boom! Crash! Bang!
It's like I'm making my colours sneeze,
In the night's breeze,
As my sparks fall like rain to the ground,
I hope my friends will be ready for their bonfire round!

Ashar Magoba (11)
Barnehurst Junior School, Erith

Whistling Demons

I am a whistling demon,
I scream as I fly through the air,
Weee! Weee!
Pretty colours fascinating the viewers,
Oh! How much they love me!

I feel so alive,
Sprinting through the sky,
Whistle, whistle!
It's the most fun I have ever had,
But I'm usually stuck in a cardboard box!

I can hear the other fireworks,
Added on to all the cheers,
Cheer, cheer!
I bet they enjoy me,
Even when I die!

Oh no! Almost time!
I've had my fame, now it's time to go,
Bang, bang!
Go the other fireworks,
Next comes me, what a short life!

I've had my glory, now I say,
Goodbye everyone, you don't care,
Scream, scream!
But this time in pain,
Ouch! It hurts, but I have no choice!

You all cheer, but imagine what it's like to have such a short life!

Ellie Martin (11)
Barnehurst Junior School, Erith

The Little Sparkler

I may not be the biggest
Or the loudest one you'll see.
But I'm a little sparkler
And everyone loves me.

I crackle and I dazzle,
For children young and old,
Everyone enjoys them
Although it's freezing cold.

I come in different colours
And can even write your name.
That's what makes a sparkler
A very fun game.

Unfortunately for sparklers
We don't last very long.
My light is now beginning to dim
And soon it will be gone.

I will shed a tear
But please don't worry children I will be back
Again next year.

Alana Dudley (10)
Barnehurst Junior School, Erith

Explodinair

Waiting all year to be opened,
Now the day has finally come,
My glorious moment has arrived,
To entertain children all ages.

The lighter is ready,
My tail is lit,
The sparks underneath me sparkle to life,
Zooming through the air like a tennis ball in play.

Whizz! Zap! Pow!
My life is nearly ending,
But what a great time I've had,
Children's laughter fills the air,
What a great sound to hear,
Especially if you're a firework.

Timothy Cross (10)
Barnehurst Junior School, Erith

Red Dragon

Bonfire Night is here at last,
I've been waiting in a box all year round,
The lid is open,
Who will they pick? *Me?*

I love their astonished faces,
As I rise into the air,
Piercing through the darkness,
But I'm sure they like me best.

When I explode gunpowder goes up my nose,
Destroying my senses,
Crash, boom, bang, wham!
I'm so colourful,
I light up the dark sky.

It's all over now,
The night is silent,
Smoke hanging in the air,
I've had my moment to shine.

Joshua Whitaker (11)
Barnehurst Junior School, Erith

That Sort Of Firework

I waited my entire life for that moment,
The happiness was overwhelming,
I was jumpy as a kangaroo,
But it was inevitable that it would happen . . .

Suddenly a hand reached in,
A wave of fear pounced on me,
But I shook it off,
I was ready!

I was placed on the mighty desert,
The fire being lit on my shell gave me a tingly sensation,
A plethora of sparkles burst out of me,
Then -I-I tripped over!

I couldn't stop myself even though I tried!
I was aimed directly at the man's legs
But he jumped out the way in the nick of time!
I slithered along the freezing grass
Like a snake watching everyone run away.
Yep, I blew it, my life was ruined.

It was inevitable that I would be that sort of firework!

Ben Hawkins (10)
Barnehurst Junior School, Erith

Chalets In The Snow

Snow as white as cauliflower
Smooth as a piece of paper
White as whipped cream
Cold as a freezer
Powdery as a flower
Cold as the coldest ice
Snow as white as the moon
Chalets covered in snow
Like tiny Toblerone bars
Floating in milkshake.

Yves Thursfield (7)
Christ Church CE Primary School, St Leonards-on-Sea

All That Silence Said

A lot of silence
But yet nothing to say
Everywhere I go, it's just silence.
There is anger in the room
But I can only feel it.
There's a depressed silence
But I can only see it.
A dead silence is so bad
And lastly, alone silence.
The worst silence ever.
All that silence leads into depression.
Silence.

Charlotte Creek (10)
Colville Primary School, Cherry Hinton

Let's Skate

Let's go and skate,
Don't be afraid,
To make a mistake.

If you fall,
Don't worry at all.
We will help you,
Then you'll say, 'Wahoo!'

Skate, skate,
Having fun,
Don't run,
Just slide along.

Skate, skate,
Do some tricks,
Like a spin,
Or twirl or swirl.

That was fun,
Let's do it again.
Unfortunately we can't,
It's over and done with.

Telma Nwakor & Shabnur Ahmed (11)
Colville Primary School, Cherry Hinton

All That Silence Said

Boring silence, angry silence, worried silence,
All that silence said,
Busy silence, surprised silence, motionless silence,
All that silence said,
Happy silence, sad silence,
All that silence dead,
Guilty silence in my heart, silence in my sleep,
Guilty silence well and truly deep,
All that silence said,
So surprised and happy silence,
You never know what to say or do,
Just say,
All that silence said,
The silence dead I shall never know,
All that silence said,
All that silence . . . dead.

Lucy Kleen (11)
Colville Primary School, Cherry Hinton

Stockings

Our stockings are as beautiful as can be,
The most beautiful stockings you will ever see.
On the sewing machines we made them,
Without much mayhem.
Carefully we created the scenes,
On top of our seams!
Now they were done,
Wow that was fun!
Although best of all,
It's mine forever more!

Alice Belham (10)
Colville Primary School, Cherry Hinton

Snow, Snow Please Don't Go

Snow, snow, snow, please don't go,
You're all so white and cold,
You set on the ground
And melt in my hand,
Snow, snow, please don't go!

Playing snowball fighting,
Making the tallest snowman,
Sledging down hills,
Let's have lots of fun!

I love to slide around,
But there's just one thing,
Please don't put snow down my top,
That's just really annoying!

Snow is white and cold,
Snow can never get old,
Because I love to play in the snow,
Snow, snow - please don't go!

Snow, snow - please don't go!

Lia Hooks (10)
Colville Primary School, Cherry Hinton

Ice Skating

Bump, boom
People falling
Bing, bang
People smiling
Splash, slosh
People learning
Ting, tang
People laughing
Toot, took
People holding
Click, clack
People trying
Ouch, oh
People bumping
Hoot, moo
People helping
Chew, chew
People eating
Flash, bong
Taking pictures
Ding, dong
People dancing
Broom, boom
People meeting
Yahooooo
Everyone is having *fun!*

Sandra Jos (10) & Sandy Salangsang (11)
Colville Primary School, Cherry Hinton

Ice Skating Madness!

We skate along
And shivering cold,
We stand out big,
Big and bold.

The sun shines down,
But the ice stays frozen,
We fall along,
Ice skating madness!

Some people are fast,
Some people are slow,
Some people don't even know
How to skate on ice and snow.

We try so hard
And have fun as well,
We sing along,
Ice skating madness.

The heart we put in
Will never be taken away,
Our skills for skating
Are brilliant every day!

Some can spin,
Some can dance,
Some can prance,
Ice skating madness!

Alice Belham (10) & Lucy Kleen (11)
Colville Primary School, Cherry Hinton

Sun

I can see the universe that surrounds me in the morning,
I can smell the swirling mist,
I can see the world below me changing at the second of movement.
It's quite dreary up here, only me and my arch enemy.
Really it's me that the world appreciates.
From when I was made, when the world was new,
I see the world changing, some good, some bad,
I am afraid that the world will forget me,
I wish I understood how people talk,
I wish that when I fall down I am not forgotten,
My name is Sun.

Lottie Bowles (10)
Cromer Junior School, Cromer

Pebble

Above me, blue skies
White, fluffy clouds
I lay on the beach and daydream
I remember getting knocked about, crashing against the waves

I am 1,000 pebbles old
I overheard someone saying they were going to throw me
I don't want anyone to find me here
I wish to stay
My name is Pebble.

Megan Purdy (11)
Cromer Junior School, Cromer

Satin Hat

I see nothing but black, I think I'm nowhere,
I touch the cobwebs, but smell the dust,
I still don't have an owner,
I am a rare sighting,
I remember all I have seen,
I am an old keepsake,
I am afraid of never seeing the sun,
I dream nothing but light,
I hear cracking stairs,
I don't understand why I haven't been worn,
I am Satin Hat.

Charity Sadler (10)
Cromer Junior School, Cromer

Watch

I can see broken chains and old earrings
I can smell rusty bronze
And I feel the blazing sun through the timid crack
I have a gold chain
I remember when I was on time
I'm afraid they'll melt me for money
I dream of seeing my father, Ben
I don't understand where the time has gone

My name is Watch.

Bethan Phillip-Pritchard (10)
Cromer Junior School, Cromer

Ben And Jerry's Ice Cream

I can see coloured boxes all around me
I taste freezing ice
I used to be loved, but no one knows I'm there
I was made five ice creams ago
I remember being defrosted in the warm microwave
I am now afraid of rotting away
I wish for someone to touch me again
I have heard the bin bags rattling
I just don't understand why nobody cares

My name is Ben and Jerry's Ice Cream.

Megan Spray (10)
Cromer Junior School, Cromer

Turtle

I live in blue, cold water,
I can see flowing seaweed bobbing about the sea,
I can smell the scent of the salty sea,
I can brush past rocks, hitting my shell
Nobody knows that I have a home under my shell
I am 42 swims old
I wish I could know why I have a shell,
I don't understand why boats crash into me,

My name is Turtle.

Hannah Austin (9)
Cromer Junior School, Cromer

Rabbit

There is rusty metal and old, rotting wood,
All I can smell is hay covered in muck,
Every day I hear people whispering,
Saying they are going to sell me,
I am 1,000 carrots old,
My hutch is full of poo,
I have a broken leg and nobody knows,
I remember being cuddled every day,
I am afraid of death and being sold,
I do not understand why they abandon me,

My name is Rabbit.

Chelsea Kerr (10)
Cromer Junior School, Cromer

Guitar

I live in the corner of a dark box room,
I can see a grandfather clock,
I can smell polish,
I have a tiny spider inside me,
I am110 plucks old,
I remember my first concert,
I am afraid that I am going to be chucked out,
I dream of having another owner,
I overheard that my owner passed away,
I do not understand that I'm still living here,

My name is Guitar.

Ellen Hedge (10)
Cromer Junior School, Cromer

Model Horse

I can see the other models standing stock still,
Staring at nothing,
I can smell the musty smell of dust,
I have lost a tiny bit of my tail,
I'm scared of being forgotten about,
I remember people staring admiringly,
I'm one hundred glances old,
I don't understand why no one looks at me anymore,

My name is Model Horse.

Eloise Garrett (9)
Cromer Junior School, Cromer

Firework

I can see people staring,
I can smell hot dogs and burgers,
I have a squeaky voice,
I am about to explode with colour,
I remember being lit alight,
I'm afraid of the dark,
But I'll soon light up the sky,
I dream of going to Mars, way up high,
I hear people aahing and oohing,
I do not understand why I have to burn out,

My name is Firework.

Naomi Court (11) & Bethany Cuff (10)
Cromer Junior School, Cromer

Tree

I can see old flowers, dead trees,
I can hear the wind howling,
I was born when the Earth was made,
I remember being young, but now I'm old,
Please let me stay here,
This is my home,

My name is Tree.

Lucy Cox (10)
Cromer Junior School, Cromer

Smile

S hiny smiles
M agnificent smiles
I f you want to you can put lipstick on your smile but only if you are a girl
L aughter is great for smiles
E xcellent smiles for the camera everyone.

Bryher Watkins (7)
Dr Walker's CE (VC) Primary School, Fyfield

Milkshake

Milkshake slurping
Sipping, sipping
Through a stripy straw
I love it to bits
Ohh yum
Scrum in my tum!

Joseph Heaney (7)
Dr Walker's CE (VC) Primary School, Fyfield

Sunny

Sun shines bright and yellow.
Just right for a swimming pool.
At night go out and have some fun
With your friends for a good laugh.
Then you will bring happiness.

Elissa Stockdale (7)
Dr Walker's CE (VC) Primary School, Fyfield

Star

In the starry sky the stars twinkle and glisten.
They are bright like a light,
Really pretty, gorgeous and beautiful.
They are nice and lovely,
So glittery and shiny.

Olivia Hussey (7)
Dr Walker's CE (VC) Primary School, Fyfield

Weather

There is lots of weather to be found.
Thunder is grey and dull, it's very lovely.
Bang, crash, wallop!
The wind cuts the cloud into weeny pieces.
It is very cold and very light.
It glitters like a thousand diamonds
When it scatters across the deep blue sky.
The wind is white and shiny,
Green leaves are dotted here and there.
The breeze is so relaxing.
You can fly your kite in this shivery weather.
Snow is so sparkly.
Snowflakes fall from fluffy clouds.
Raindrops fall from the sky, filling the air with joy.
Rain and sun makes a rainbow.
The shades of red, orange, yellow, green, blue, indigo and violet
Fill the world with happiness.
Sunsets are beautiful.
It turns clouds to purple and blue.
People love weather.

Alice Bennett (7)
Dr Walker's CE (VC) Primary School, Fyfield

Volcano

If you see a volcano it is very high.
It will make a lot of noise.
Bang, bang, bang!

This brown thing might look good
But it's not, believe me!
I always tell the truth.
Bang, bang, bang!

Dripping, dripping, dripping.
This is very bad.
It's fire.
Bang, bang, bang!

This is bad.
The fire is coming.
Argh!
Bang, bang, bang!

Jack Langston (8)
Dr Walker's CE (VC) Primary School, Fyfield

Wolves

All wolves love to howl at the moon.
All wolves love to eat rabbits and things that are nice.
All wolves love to race and run to the nearest tree to rub their paws on.
All wolves love to jump up and down like they've got the World Cup.
All wolves love to pull sleighs all around the world again and again.

Ionie Heppel (8)
Dr Walker's CE (VC) Primary School, Fyfield

Hairstyles

You can have bunches
You can have pigtails
You can have plaits
You can have it down
You can have it wild
You can have it straight
You can have it frizzy
You can have it curly
You can have a bob
You can have it long
You can have it spiky
You can put hairspray in it
You can have gel in it
You can have ribbons
You can have bobbles
How would you like your hair?

Harley Harris (7)
Dr Walker's CE (VC) Primary School, Fyfield

Calf The Giraffe Who Got Hit On The Head By A Tree

Calf the giraffe was very tall
But others call him Mr Small.
Calf says he has lots of might
But always has an excuse like the sun is too bright.
One night he sneaked out
But his parents say at night he shouldn't be about.
Just at that time a tree whacked him on the head,
The next minute he was dead.
In the morning all the animals found something on the ground,
They found a dead giraffe on the ground.

Sona Elonge (7)
Goodrington School, Hornchurch

Blood And Guts

In the quiet dark night
A cat stood in sight.
But the still cat was dead,
As it had no head.

'Twas because of a ghost
Who loved to boast.
Let me tell you the story,
Even though it's gory.

Bat was still,
Lying on top of a hill.
Suddenly he stood,
He was Dracula wearing a hood.

Whoosh!
Went a noise from inside a bush.
Hoot, hoot, went a noise,
Which couldn't give Drac joys.

Then beady-eyed Drac,
Found a small cat.
Ghost finally said,
'Do you want to eat his head?'

'I'd love to!'
Then Drac shouted, 'Boo!'
Drac got Cat's head
And Ghost turned red.

A small little witch,
Put Cat's head in the ditch.
Then Ghost hitched
A ride with bewitched
Storybook crooks,
Who gave dirty looks.

Aleera Ewan (8)
Goodrington School, Hornchurch

Flowers

On the soft, silk grass on which they lay,
Gently in the breeze they sway
And from the dew of break of dawn,
As beautiful as a newborn fawn.

Light and wonderful, colourful and bright,
Twinkling cheerfully in the night,
Lovely as they glitter and sparkle,
I think flowers are truly remarkable!

Gracefully dancing away,
While looking up at the sun's ray
And when they start to drink some rain,
It tastes as sweet as a candy cane.

They love to dance,
As I leap and prance
And it makes me ever so jolly,
Just like my little Cindy dolly!

To be a flower is my dream,
If I could, I would beam
And to join in with their swaying game,
How I wish a flower to be my name!

And now I feel like telling you my favourite part,
Which puts deep love into my heart
And slowly, slowly they start to bloom,
Where they find new space and room.

Tami Olorunfemi (9)
Goodrington School, Hornchurch

It's Cold

It's cold,
It's cold,
It's shivering here.
It's cold,
It's cold,
Let's run to the pier.

It's cold,
It's cold,
It's freezing now.
It's cold,
It's cold,
It's cold.

So they all declare,
To go home and prepare.
A nice hot meal
To fill them up
And make them warm again.

Regina Johnson (8)
Goodrington School, Hornchurch

Colours

Colours can be brown, colours can be grey
Colours I see nearly every day
You can find them in a book if you would like to take a look
And that's two reasons about colours

Colours up high in the sky
Colours down all over the town
I see colours on my purple and pink gown
And that's four reasons about colours
I like yellow and grey and I wear it every day!

Bethel Uduojie (7)
Goodrington School, Hornchurch

My Rabbit's Life

My rabbit's life:
there's so little
to it,
so little
to it.

She crunches the iron bar
and decides for the ninety-ninth
billionth time
that she just can't
eat it.

My rabbit's life:
there's so little
to it,
so little
to it.

It's about the most exciting
life in the world,
if I only knew it.
She hops and she eats and she drinks
and lives a life of luxury.

She nibbles and she chews.
This process, she repeats.

My rabbit's life:
there's so little
to it,
so little
to it.

Caroline Enaw (11)
Goodrington School, Hornchurch

Little Miss Muffet

Little Miss Muffet
Sat on her tuffet
But not eating her curds and whey
Along came a spider
As big as a glider
With a message from her mum -
If you don't eat your lunch
I'll give you a punch!
So she made the spider
Sit down beside her
And force fed it till it burst!
When she got home she rubbed her tum
And said to her mum,
'Yum! Yum!'

Britani Mursell (11)
Goodrington School, Hornchurch

Crunchy Munchy The Chocolate Bar

Crunchy Munchy was a chocolate bar
He likes to ride in his little red car
He plays all night
He plays all day
From early morning
Till early sunset comes today
He likes the park and goes there now
He likes the animals which are the black and white cows
One time it was hot
And he started to melt a lot
And suddenly melted to the ground
And that was the end of Crunchy Munchy
And his sound.

Megan Weeden (10)
Goodrington School, Hornchurch

Cupcakes

C akes are yummy too,
U nable to resist
P ink and blue and lots of different coloured cakes,
C upcakes, cupcakes,
A cup of tea and a piece of cake,
K eep them safe in case your brother or sister eats them,
E at with joy,
S ay, 'Cupcakes are yummy!'

Molly Whittaker (9)
Great Abington Primary School, Great Abington

Unicorns

His nose as soft as silk,
His fur as white as newly laid snow,
His mane and tail glowing gold in the moonlight,
His eyes glow fiercely as he neighs goodbye,
He leaves a trail of fairy dust through the midnight sky,
Only I can see him though,
If you want to know I'll tell you why,
Because he's my special unicorn!

Leilani Towler (9)
Great Abington Primary School, Great Abington

The Man That Lived In Jamaica

There once was a man that lived in Jamaica
He wanted a job as a baker
He burnt his bread
It was hard as lead
And now he delivers the paper.

Luke Silcock (9)
Great Abington Primary School, Great Abington

Castles And Weapons

C astles with walls so high I think they tickle the sky
A nd a moat as murky as a marsh
S o round it never ends just enormous murky water
T he gate and drawbridge fall and go bang!
L ow ranking peasants treated like animals
E verywhere soldiers with spears glinting gold
S tores selling meat, vegetables, weapons and armour

A lways selling really well
N ever going out of stock
D oing brilliantly in business

W hat looks a fight has broken out
'E eek,' he screams as the opponent pulls out a sword
A fter that he was arrested
'P oor man,' I say as he is taken away on a stretcher
O nly to be burnt
N o funeral
S o that's why I don't want to live in a castle.

Tom Ricketts (9)
Great Abington Primary School, Great Abington

Mr Bug

Mr Bug is really lazy
Not fun but very crazy
He sings a song
It's really long
And he takes too long putting his shoes on

Mr Bug is really cold
He looks like icky mould
Great like cake
That he just baked
That's what I call Mr Bug

Mr Bug is really sleepy
Not fat but really creepy
Time for bed
Sleeps on his head
This is Mr Bug.

Harry Mallows (10)
Great Abington Primary School, Great Abington

When I Go To The Beach

When I go to the beach I hear a band
And I dig in the sand
I dug so far I reached New Zealand
Then Mum got me a burger, when she came back she looked up
And I said hello
And then I saw a panda called Po
We were best mates for ever and we went home in a UFO.

Sam Logan (9)
Great Abington Primary School, Great Abington

Sock Monster

S ocks on the floor will get him out of bed
O ver and over again he'll hit you on the head
C link, clank, clonk he hits you, he bites until you pick them up
K ick him and punch him, just doesn't work, so pick your socks off the floor

M um comes in and screams out again
O ver and over again he'll come back again
N ever leave your socks on the floor
S itting down or standing up he'll come and get you again
T omorrow you'll remember don't leave your socks on the floor
E very day he'll come and get you again
R emember don't leave your socks on the floor.

Harry Kilcommons (9)
Great Abington Primary School, Great Abington

Vicious Vikings

V ikings are very scary, they are as strong as a bulldozer
I t makes my spine shiver and the beards smell of guts and liver
C an anyone bear the smell of rotten guts and poo?
I f you try to fight one I wouldn't if I were you
O ur armies don't stand a chance against those smelly foes
U nderneath their hairy bodies are big spots of green
S o if you see a Viking just *run and scream!*

V ikings are a fierce bunch
I t makes people scream, even the Romans
K ill them and lots of guts and blood will come out
I ll people catch it from Vikings
N ow let's kill them
G uts, blood, brains and hearts that's all Vikings see
S o if you see a Viking run!

Cameron Foo (9)
Great Abington Primary School, Great Abington

Colours

C olours are everywhere
O ver hills and in the air
L ike flying horses over your head
O ver come the rainbow sun that flies around in your bed
U nder the sea you will see how colours are everywhere
R ainbows fly around the clouds catching rain as they pass
S unny weather here we come like the sun in a bun.

Verity Finlayson (9)
Great Abington Primary School, Great Abington

The Flea That Jumped In My Tea

Once I was drinking tea
And then I swallowed a flea.
He jumped down my throat,
Made a noise like a goat
And then he shouted in me.
He shouted hello
And played the cello
The flea that jumped in my tea.
He whispered goodbye
And started to cry.
He jumped out my throat,
Made a noise like a stoat
And then he waved at me.

Sammy Ellis (9)
Great Abington Primary School, Great Abington

The Stars - Haiku

Sparkling, shimmering,
Shining, glistening, gleaming,
Flashing, twinkling stars.

Olivia Crawley (10)
Great Abington Primary School, Great Abington

Candy Sweet Leaves

I thought of a tree with candy sweet leaves
And it popped up in front of me
It wasn't that queer
Because I saw it appear
But then wasn't that clear
And then it became very sincere
Because a tree
Had just materialised in front of me
Why didn't I know it was just a show?
And nothing had happened out of the ordinary.

Joanna Cloherty (9)
Great Abington Primary School, Great Abington

The Harpy

Most people think the harpy is ugly
And mean, but they are wrong . . .
Once a snowy night I was still awake,
Upon my window sill sat a harpy red and green
Eagle with glowing eyes so green
I opened my window and got on the harpy's back, flew away
I saw a wild horse galloping across a beach, deer frolicking in a river
Then he stopped on a cliff and gave me a statue of him . . .
Now every snowy night I fly with him!

Eiléanór Crilly (9)
Great Abington Primary School, Great Abington

Humpty-Dumpty Went To Mars

Humpty-Dumpty went to Mars
To buy some yummy chocolate bars,
When he got there, they were all sold out,
So then he started to shout out . . .
'I have come all the way to Mars,
To buy some yummy chocolate bars
And now I'm here and you're all sold out,
So now I have started to shout.'
So Humpty-Dumpty left Mars
Without any yummy chocolate bars,
So he went back to Earth,
Then pulled up his Grandpa's turf,
What a naughty egg from the Planet Earth!

Travis Parr (10)
Great Abington Primary School, Great Abington

The Holy Treasure

Once I was walking down a windy lane,
when I saw a tree.
I looked at it, it looked at me
and then it decided to speak to me.
'Oh please brave boy
can you come to my aid and rescue me?'
'Oh yes,' I said for I knew, the burden of this tree,
it was protecting the holy treasure, from the evil queen.
So the tree moved its roots, a little to the side
and then finally it revealed to me a shabby trapdoor.
It was small and black and dirty as if eager to hide,
and then I opened it up a little and then I went inside.
It was dark and damp and dirty, when I went inside.
The walls were pressing on me like an eagle on his prey.
But finally I found the place where the treasure lay.
But guarding it was a giant flea just waiting to bite me.
I sat on the floor next to a giant door to think of a plan,
and finally in a blinding flash the answer came to me.
I threw some meat across the room and as I had expected,
there came the flea lumbering across the room to pick up the food
I had left in it.
I dashed forwards towards the treasure and before the flea could catch me
I had the treasure in my arms and so I know from this day,
that the tree will forever be grateful to me.

Simon Herberholz (10)
Great Abington Primary School, Great Abington

The Bogey Monster

He came over and tried to grab me with his green sticky hands.
He came over and tried to whack me with his ginormous fist.
He came over and tried to push me with his huge round belly.
He came over and tried to kick me with his slimy leg.

Joe Ryen (8)
Great Abington Primary School, Great Abington

The Monster Under My Bed

As my mum says goodnight to me
And when she switches off the light,
I pull my quilt over my face to hide me from the monster,
Sweat drools down my face like Formula 1's racing,
Outside my house, trees clack and tap and smack my window,
The wind whistles there and then like a ghost down the road,
This makes me nervous,
I want to scream but the fear holds me frozen,
Like Antarctica has moved in my room,
I wonder why the monster chose me to make me feel like a baby.
1 o'clock, six hours till morning, I cannot wait, I shut my eyes
And try to forget but the mattress is moving!
There it is, 'the monster under my bed'!
I cannot stand this any more, I get out of bed,
Get a pillow then turn on the light,
The monster creeps out under my bed as my jaws start to drop,
The monster is spotty, got hairy fur like knives poking out,
Its teeth are bloody, I step back twice
And hit the monster very hard . . .
But it did no good, he tries to eat me. I wake up . . .
Dream or reality?
It is morning, I go downstairs to watch some TV,
But in my wardrobe red eyes glare through the gap
Waiting for the next night . . .

Alexander Van Dort (10)
Guyhirn CE (VC) Primary School, Guyhirn

The Escape From My Fantasy

As I walk up the stairs
I think about my nightmares,
Then I get to my door
And think about the lion's roar,
And as my mum walks step by step to bed,
I feel I'm a prisoner kept.
It's my fantasy what should I do?
Where can I go? And what can I do?
I try to fight the sleep
But before I know it, my duvet has covered me, 'm too deep!
The lion is chasing me through the Sahara Desert,
And then suddenly I bump into a peasant.
Help! Help! I'm falling down,
Now here comes a man with a golden crown.
It's my fantasy what should I do?
Where can I go? And what can I do?
Suddenly . . . suddenly it goes dark
So I light my candle with a spark,
Here comes the lion, he's growling loud,
When I find myself touching a cloud.
Then I hear my mum pick up her cup,
Finally I've woken up!
It's my fantasy, it's ended well.
Now I feel like I'm out of my prison cell.

Brooke Jade Lee (9)
Guyhirn CE (VC) Primary School, Guyhirn

Monster Under My Bed

Monster under my bed
Huge thighs
Ugly, big eyes
Monster under my bed.

Monster under my bed
He sweeps with a broom
He makes my toy go *boom!*
Monster out of my room.

Monster never going to come back
Monster never going to come back
If he comes back he will get a big smack
Monster never going to come back.

Max Paton (9)
Guyhirn CE (VC) Primary School, Guyhirn

My Pet Paul

My pet Paul is so cool.
He has a pool and likes to drool.
He eats fish on a dish with his mum called Slish.
He went on a date with his mate called Kate.

He sleeps at day with his sister May.
He's awake at night with his brother Fright.
My dad went mad when he was bad.
He said sorry to Molly and Polly.
'He is so silly,' said Millie and Billy.
So his name is Paul and he is so cool.

Becky Cawley (10)
Guyhirn CE (VC) Primary School, Guyhirn

Home Time!

Finally it's home time, grab our bags and run time,
Throw our books on the floor, jump out of the door,
Slipping on the ground, now finding our way around,
Running to our car door, slipping, sliding a little more,
Tell our mum to hurry up as she turns the gear up,
Because it is the end of term, Christmas time will soon alarm,
Sliding to the front gate, hurry up Mum we're gonna be late!
Slip on our party clothes, put nail varnish on our toes,
Running down the street, there my friends I meet,
For there's a party going on and it feels like a prom!

Emily Gratton (10)
Guyhirn CE (VC) Primary School, Guyhirn

The Environment

The state of the mess they have made, is quite atrocious I am afraid to say!
Bins empty, pavements full, oh what is the point? Everything is dull.
Some people are lazy, I have to say,
So why can't you just follow the rules, like everyone else so nothing can fall?
Cans in rivers embedded in ground, dangerous, not safe and sound,
Don't snigger at litter, because it's important to not, to save all,
People have made littering a disgrace to our human race so please stop now!

Jenson Tebbs (10)
Guyhirn CE (VC) Primary School, Guyhirn

My Family And Me

My family's really caring but can sometimes be mad
But then at times I can be really bad,
I can be really smiley when dinner comes
With lovely coloured cupcakes and chocolate covered thumbs.
When it comes to bedtime I hate that time, I just don't want to go
So when my parents go to bed I stay up really late but they don't know.
In the morning I like to play volleyball and football
I wish I could play these games forever but then I trip and fall.

Charlotte Angela Richardson (10)
Guyhirn CE (VC) Primary School, Guyhirn

Game Over

Today I played 'Donkey Kong'
But he had a real big pong
Then I sung him a soothing song
But he had a shower
Then he had almighty power
But then he climbed the Eiffel Tower
Then I told him to stop and listen
But he saw his friend from Lisbon
Then he shouted his dog called Gibson
Then I said I have had enough of being treated like garbage
Then the DS spoke
Game Over!

George Napier (10)
Guyhirn CE (VC) Primary School, Guyhirn

I Went To The Moon

I went to the moon with a kangaroo, I don't think you understand
Because going to the moon with a kangaroo is simply just mad!
It gave me a hug and a cool looking slug
and off we went with a boom!
A spark here and there and a whoosh everywhere
and that's how we got to the moon.
It's cold up here, I can't quite hear,
for there is a moon rock in my ear.

Hebe May Baker (10)
Guyhirn CE (VC) Primary School, Guyhirn

Never-Ending Reading Fun

They take you to a different world
When your eyes are upon the page
When someone stops you reading fast it angers you with rage!
Be the person on the page among that very book
Stare forever
Be there forever
Reading till this book is done, it's the never-ending reading fun.

They take you to a different world
When your head is deep in the page
When someone takes your book away it angers you with rage!
Help the person on the page among that very book
Be there forever
Read there forever
It's the never-ending reading fun!

Jessica Goode (11)
Guyhirn CE (VC) Primary School, Guyhirn

Dancing

D ancing moves are like stars, you can't touch them but they will lead you to your destiny.
A rt form skilful and fun.
N ever the same step, it's all confusing at times when you go up a level you will find the steps are much harder than normal.
C omplicated steps and moves to learn and practise over and over again.
I t gives me a lift when I am sad.
N ervous when I go on stage but then transports me to another world.
G oals, to go to stage school, get in a higher level in ballet and tap and jazz.

Elisha Burgess (9)
Guyhirn CE (VC) Primary School, Guyhirn

Monday Morning

Monday morning is so boring,
It's nearly break time, yeah!
Today is maths, that is great,
But I feel English will be my fate!
It's nearly lunch - I'm so starving!
Let's have a chit-chat with my friend Marvin.
Miss a few hours
That's the bell - better go!

Natasha Young (10)
Guyhirn CE (VC) Primary School, Guyhirn

Dreaming Of Candyland

If the world was made of candy,
I would call the one in the gingerbread house Mandy.

With lollies and Smarties used as stepping stones,
If the world was simply like this no one would moan.

Icing and chocolate bars,
Mmmmm, I'm not sure if there will be cars.

It's my dream,
Sitting there eating cookies and cream.

Rolos and Polos I love them all,
Where are my mates?
Oh look they're swimming in the toffee pool, how cool.

I wake up from my candyfloss dream
And I found out I was not eating cookies and cream.

But sleeping cosily in my sweet little bed.

Melissa Jones (9)
Guyhirn CE (VC) Primary School, Guyhirn

Pixies

They are in my garden,
I know they are.
Cautiously, silently,
Though I still hear them from afar.

Their purple hair on their small heads.
They have bright make-up and neon-coloured clothes.
Majestic, shy and beautiful creatures are what they are . . .
They are pixies.

Naomi Ugoh (10)
La Salette RC Primary School, Rainham

The Funky Beat!

I looked at the man
and the man looked back.
He paralysed me
and my vision went black.

Next thing I knew
I was on the street,
and had to get up
to this funky beat.

Which went a little like this!

A hip hop
hibi dibi jibi.
You don't stop
cos I'm a bit flimsy!

Tommy Nye (10)
La Salette RC Primary School, Rainham

Steve The Superhero

I'm Steve the superhero
and you simple won't believe
the superpowers I possess
by merely being Steve.

My smile can crack a mirror
and my breath can make you faint.
And when I take my socks off
it's been known to smell worse than paint.

The smell of my mighty armpits
can make a grown man cry.
A single burp can make you want
to crawl away and die.

The bad guys know it's hopeless,
so they all get up and leave
whenever they get a sniff of me . . .
the superhero Steve.

Wyan Reid (11)
La Salette RC Primary School, Rainham

The Fire

Crackling, crackling, crackling,
All the night through.
The fire's burning around us,
What are we going to do?

Sparks of fire flying everywhere,
Like shooting stars.
The fire is getting bigger,
I'm sure they can see it from Mars!

The circle of Hell surrounds us!
We step out we burn,
We stay in - who knows?
I'm sure we'll learn.

Drifting all around,
The smoke fills the air.
It spreads across the land,
Without a care.

Crackling, crackling, crackling,
All the night through.
The fire's burning around us,
What are we going to do?

Emma Kearney (10)
La Salette RC Primary School, Rainham

Fire

F lutters high in the night sky,
I nfernos beyond the horizon.
R etreats slowly back home,
E very fire brings good or bad.

Busola Egunnike (11)
La Salette RC Primary School, Rainham

Autumn Among Us

The frosty breeze, autumn has begun.
Coloured trees, red, amber and gold;
Hats and gloves taken out and wrapped up
With the crunching leaves under my feet.

Sat by the warming fire with my hot tea,
Walking through the forest for conkers to play.
Squirrels scampering around unearthing nuts;
With the crunching leaves under my feet.

Exploring the forest for conkers to play,
Summer waves goodbye, countdown to Christmas.
Stormy clouds threaten the sky, dark at six, early nights
With the crunching leaves under my feet.

The last leaves grasping on branches of trees.
Apples picked fresh, cooked into crumble.
Halloween, scary costumes, trick or treat!
With the crunching leaves under my feet.

Autumn is among us!

Kieran Ratnayake (11)
La Salette RC Primary School, Rainham

The Water Nymph

You hide in the waters risen,
As I seek to draw near,
Often I hear you,
But now more faint and clear.
You are bold and outspoken,
But sweet in a way,
You want to be left unknown,
So I leave you on your way.

Chloe Tiwo (10)
La Salette RC Primary School, Rainham

I've Seen A Place . . .

I've seen a place where wild daisies grow
And fairies sleep in the petals of a rose,
Always at dusk they start their flight,
Just to have fun in shadows of the moonlight.

Through the trees like lines of light,
Blinding those who see that sight,
You could refer to them as fireflies,
Live for years and never die.

Queen Denettia, she rules Fairy Land,
Living life, looking grand.
I've seen a place where wild daisies grow
And fairies sleep in the petals of a rose.

Ellie Noad (10)
La Salette RC Primary School, Rainham

Autumn Days

Autumn smells like hot chocolate and fireworks.
Trees take off their coat of leaves,
Waving their bare branches at me.
The golden leaves dancing around my feet.

As wind pushes away golden gilt leaves,
The wind blasts through my hair.
A cold gust touches my face.

Animals collecting their food all day.
Put on coats because fall is here.

The crisp of crunchy leaves.
Gilt and flashing orange.

Molly Last (10)
La Salette RC Primary School, Rainham

There's A Little World In My Back Garden

There's a little world in my back garden,
A secret I have to tell,
Little daisy fairies,
Who I know ever so well.

They pounce gracefully from daisy to daisy,
Pink, white and red,
Little daisies fly from tree to tree
And one even bounced on my knee!

With their snowy white dresses with scarlet ribbons,
They look ever so cute!
But in the winter they wear their tiny, fluffy mittens,
Looking like little baby kittens.

These little daisies have such big hearts!
And very much like to eat their special cherry tart,
After supper has finished they fly around the wood,
Saying goodnight to everyone!
I would go with them if I could.

They spring from leaf to leaf then hop into bed,
With the comfort of the warm, pink daisy petals
And the trees singing a soft melody,
Every little daisy fairy asleep, no one in sight,
They wake up in the morning, with the sun burning bright.

There's a little world in my back garden,
A secret you have to keep,
Remember the little daisy fairies,
Long, in their deep little sleep!

Katy Burke (11)
La Salette RC Primary School, Rainham

What Has Happened?

The reckless pollution,
Does anyone have a simple solution?
The cars go past with a loud beep
And just look at that rubbish heap!

The factories produce steam
And I hate the gangster team!
The broken benches
And the deep trenches
Are always so bad.

The trees are cut down
And that gives me a frown.
We do it for paper on which we scribble
And then we feel the picture needs to be tripled.

My favourite time on the streets
Is when it is as quiet as a mouse.
All the lights are turned off,
Peace, finally.

Oliver Slatford (11)
Loyola Preparatory School, Buckhurst Hll

Africa

A frica is boiling
F rogs there are
R afiki is funny
I love Africa
C ircle of life
A frica hosted the 2010 World Cup.

Christopher Petre (9)
Notley Green Primary School, Great Notley

The Lion King Rocks

T he circle of life
H yenas
E lephants

L eopard
I ndependent
O ther animals eat other animals
N ew life

K ing Mufasa
I guana
N ewborns
G iraffe

R hino
O ther animals work as a team
C heetah
K angaroos
S nake.

Lucy Elliott (10)
Notley Green Primary School, Great Notley

Africa

A nimals are wild
F rogs are green and slimy
R hinos are grey and stiff
I like them all I think
C reepy-crawlies in the dark
A rgh, a spider.

Arran Stuart (10)
Notley Green Primary School, Great Notley

Swallowing Sorrow

He dragged what was left of his belongings through the darkness,
He felt the cool fabric of his shorts rub gently against his knees -
The feeling comforted him.
He wearily pulled his hat over his ears, protecting him from the strong wind whispering the last words Lesley had said.
When he reached the inn nearby, he swiped the single lock of grey hair out of his eyes and gulped the clean air.
The first thing he saw was the smiling landlady, her eyes glossing in the dimmed light,
Smoke was filling the room from the cigarettes hanging out of the drunken fools' mouths,
'One room, for as long as I can stay,' he told the landlady, reaching out to receive the key.
'Certainly, here we go . . . ' She handed the key lightly, almost knowing he was grieving.
He lugged himself up the creaky stairs and entered his room, fiddling impatiently with the key.
When he got in the room he sat on the end of the bed, covered in light blue linen,
He took off his heavy green overcoat and revealed his prized possession, a grey plait of hair,
Then gently, he sobbed to himself in memory of his dear, late wife lost minutes ago.

Evie Stoneman (11)
Notley Green Primary School, Great Notley

Fred

There was a boy called Fred
Who was in search of a bed
He went to Dreams
In Milton Keynes

Then Fred was dead
In his bed
That he bought from Dreams
In Milton Keynes.

Charlie Long (11)
Notley Green Primary School, Great Notley

A Man Called Fred!

There was a young man called Fred,
Who really hurt his head!
He went purple and blue
And fell down the loo
So that was the end of Fred!

Lillian James (11)
Notley Green Primary School, Great Notley

The Lion King

There was once a lion called Scar.
The most evil lion by far.
Mufasa dies in the stampede.
The animals become in need.
Simba saved the day, killed Scar.
Everyone shouted hooray!

Victoria Smith (9)
Notley Green Primary School, Great Notley

The Doctor Who TARDIS Rhyme

When the TARDIS lands on the moon
Get ready to get back in soon
Or you will be sent off to your doom
When the TARDIS is travelling in time and space
Don't forget to insult the alien race
Instead of sitting there doing your lace
When the Doctor lands on Gallifrey
He will meet the Time Lords face to face.

Callum Beedie (9)
Notley Green Primary School, Great Notley

A World Of War

Bombs are flying, bullets are firing.
Many men are dead, they got shot in the head.
We're living in a world of war.

As Hitler marched the Nazis on,
The war will go on and on,
As the airforce fly up high,
They kiss their wives a pleasant goodbye.
We're living in a world of war.

As Churchill makes his wise plan,
Hitler thinks he is the man,
As the Russians help us win the war,
We left Germany very poor.
We are living in a world of war.

Billy Dryden (10)
Notley Green Primary School, Great Notley

The Lion King

The Lion King is so cool
That evil Scar is such a fool.
The lion I mentioned earlier, Scar
Is going to be the evilest lion by far.
When Mufasa owned the pride land
Not one little thing was bad.
But Pride Rock will be in a shock
When everything falls down
And you will look like a clown.
Far away in another land
There is Simba lying in the sand.
He should get back fast enough
Before Pride Rock gets very tough.

Harry Fraser (9)
Notley Green Primary School, Great Notley

Nature Is . . .

Nature is beautiful,
It is what makes us live.
Nature is beautiful,
Beauty is all it seems to give.

Nature is wonderful,
It is what makes the world go round.
Nature is wonderful,
But is spoilt when litter is on the ground.

Nature is brilliant,
It is nice to be around.
Nature is brilliant,
My dog digs it up because she is a greyhound!

Nature is amazing,
But it's sometimes not what it seems.
Nature is amazing,
But not when hurricanes tear through the streets.

Nature is the world,
It is so cool.
Nature is the world,
If you didn't like it you would be a fool!

Polly Temple (9)
Notley Green Primary School, Great Notley

Baa Baa Black Sheep's Twist

Yo, yo black sheep have you any wool?
Excuse me but I'm already cool,
I'm sheered to my skin,
Go ask my brother Finn.

Yo, yo black sheep have you any wool?
Have you any eyes at all?
I'm covered from head to toe,
I've even topped it with a nice red bow,
Not one single hair is leaving my head,
Go ask my brother Fred.

Yo, yo black sheep have you any wool?
No, I feel like a fool,
I'm freezing cold
And everything's starting to mould,
With no central heating,
The sheering master is the one for beating
And if you want to catch up with the sheering master,
You better run a little faster.

No, no, no,
I'm the sheering master and that is so,
I'm going to have you for my dinner,
Because I'm getting thinner,
No Sir,
No Sir,
We are easy to keep
And you're making us weep,
Besides we don't have any fleas,
Yes, but you'll taste nice with peas!

Holly Clarke (10)
Notley Green Primary School, Great Notley

The Tears Of A Clown

Clowns are supposedly happy
And always dippy, doppy, dappy.
But sometimes clowns
Have the frowns.

It's a very sad sight to see,
As clowns are usually full of glee.
Sometimes, when they are woeful
Their eyes are extremely doleful.

I'm an upbeat person
But it really gets me down,
When I go to the circus and see
The tears of a clown.

Tilly Kilkelly (10)
Notley Green Primary School, Great Notley

Summer

The leaves had just turned bright green,
The flowers had just been seen,
The sun dazzled like a wonderful dream,
Everyone had an ice cream,
Even the Queen.

Tasnim Rahman (11)
Notley Green Primary School, Great Notley

World War Two

In World War Two
Women had the jobs
All the men were fighting
There was rationing in the shops.

In World War Two
Women worked
Little to cook with
Only 50g of butter, 50g of lard.

Air raid sirens ringing
Such a fearsome sound
Hitler's bombs crashing
Down on England's green ground.

Evacuees with shaking knees
Labels on their chests
With tears dripping down their cheeks
Wave goodbye, dressed in their best.

In World War Two
It was hard to live
Everyone tried to do their best
With courage and bravery they did give.

Isobel Hooper (10)
Oaklands School, Loughton

About Me

A sweet, lovely girl.
Long golden hair.
Dark brown eyes.
A very small nose.
Little, sweet ears.
I love animals.
I love my family
And they love me.
I am the sweetest girl in the world.

Alana Cooper (7)
Oaklands School, Loughton

Evacuees

E vacuate is what we had to go from the bulky, bursting bombs.
V ery sad because my mum and dad would miss me
twenty-four hours a day.
A udiences of people gathered round to say farewell
to their children like me.
C oming from everywhere, *choo-choo*, the train is finally here.
U pset, I did not want to go, I would miss my dog.
E ntering the train, children tired, weak and terrified.
What would happen next?
E ating hardly anything on the train, finally we arrive at our destination.
S omebody picks me and we go to her house,
I have a good feeling.

Amrit Minhas (10)
Oaklands School, Loughton

School Trip To The London Eye

It wasn't moving at all when I first saw the Eye
My stomach was tight, I was going to die!
Move up Emily, I'm going to cry!
I want to see us flying in the sky.

See that tree with greeny leaves?
See those tiny kids that look like ants?
See the park where we'll have lunch?
Look at the swings that look like wings!
Trying to see such things to do
Taking photos of all that we do
Telling teachers what a fabulous day
I never want to go home, I pray.

Slowly coming down from the pod
People grow bigger than a dog
I step out on the ground
My dream is over I have found.

Katia Brookes (10)
Oaklands School, Loughton

The London Eye

Once upon a rhyme
In a land far away,
Some school kids
Went on a trip that day.

To the London Eye,
We stepped on board,
But after a while
I got quite bored!

We got to the top
In our thick glass pod,
I felt like I
Was close to God.

I ran around
And jumped with glee,
I think I could almost
See the sea!

Slowly and steadily
We came down,
Then my feet
Touched the ground.

I prayed to God
And said, 'Thank you!'
For safely returning
From that view.

I felt absurd,
I really didn't want
To be a bird.
And yet I'd flown!

Elizabeth Davis (9)
Oaklands School, Loughton

V & A

We went on a school trip
It was very cool
We visited the V & A Museum
It was wonderful.

We dressed up as Victorian girls
And in some paintings there were white pearls
Many paintings were quite weird
And most of them had short beards.

We went round to the stage
To see things from the Victorian age
We did a Victorian show
Which everyone loved so.

We had lunch and had yummy food
That was also good
We went to the gift shop
And tried to spend a lot!

We only had five pounds
And we had to look around
Very good, yes it was
All day long, we had fun.

We all had so much fun
But it had to come
The end of the day
Time goes so fast.

We all went on the coach
Back to school, off we go
All we remember
Was lots of fun.

Megan Christie (9)
Oaklands School, Loughton

Animal Lover

I'm a . . .
Dog chaser
Dog lover
Dog kisser
Dog walker
Dog lover.
I'm a . . .
Cat chaser
Cat lover
Cat kisser
Cat walker
Cat lover.
I'm a . . .
Rabbit chaser
Rabbit lover
Rabbit kisser
Rabbit walker
Rabbit lover.
I'm a . . .
Hamster chaser
Hamster lover
Hamster kisser
Hamster walker
Hamster lover.
I'm an . . .
Animal lover
Animal kisser
Animal chaser
Animal walker
Forever.

Mizgin Dicle Kaya (8)
Oaklands School, Loughton

About Me

Scooter adorer
Pizza cruncher
Dog and cat adorer
Mummy hugger
School adorer
Watch wearer
Science doer
Camping lover
Chocolate adorer
Crisp muncher
Spider hater
Ladybird lover.

Sophie Young (7)
Oaklands School, Loughton

My Dog

Ball catcher
Face licker
Tail chaser
High jumper
Food lover
Loud barker
Cat chaser
Water lover
Cat hater
Rabbit chaser
Biscuit lover
Girl lover.

Ella Rebecca Irwin (8)
Oaklands School, Loughton

All About Me!

Dog lover
Monkey lover
Horse adorer
Cat liker
Puppy adorer
Pony stroker
Horse wanter
Milk liker
Party lover
Chocolate lover
Biscuit adorer
Horse rider.

Amy Byrne (8)
Oaklands School, Loughton

Cats

Food lover
Ball player
Fish catcher
Mouse hunter
Streets roamer
Water licker
Rabbit chaser
Long liver
Frisbee fetcher
Bed hairer
Dog hater
Story reader
Pencil scratcher
Stranger meeter.

Grace Gadeke (7)
Oaklands School, Loughton

The Song Of The Elephant

Your tusks for our ivory statues.
Your feet for our stable stools.
You trumpet in the green, great land.
Elephant, I heard you calling.
Great elephant, grieving for your life,
Grieving for your kind, great heart.
I knew how we would use your dying.
You trumpet in the green, great land.
Elephant, I heard you grieving.
You trumpet, call and rumble.
Your heart can beat like thunder and lightning.
We would make you dumb.
Your tusks for our ivory statues.
Your feet for our stable stools.

Isabelle Dickinson (9)
Oaklands School, Loughton

The Song Of The Turtle

Your meat for our soup
Your eggs for our food.

Majestic creature in the sea.

Turtle, I heard you crying.
I heard how we would use your dying.

Your meat for our soup
Your eggs for our food.

Beautiful creature in the sea.
Turtle, I heard moaning, wailing, sobbing.

I heard your heart beating rhythmically
Like a tapping finger.

We would make you dumb.

Your meat for our soup
Your eggs for our food.

Gabriella Kounnis (8)
Oaklands School, Loughton

The Song Of The Turtle

Your meat for our soup
Your eggs for our food

Slow little thing in the sea
Turtle I heard you crying

Turtle, weeping for your life
Crying for your kind
How we would use your dying

Your meat for our soup
Your eggs for our food

Beautiful little thing in the sea
Turtle, I heard you mourning

You make a weeping noise in the sea
Turtle I heard you wailing and sobbing at night

I heard your rhythmic heart
Beating like a drum

I would make you dumb

Your meat for our soup
Your eggs for our food.

Ava Moore (8)
Oaklands School, Loughton

The Song Of The Elephant

Your tusks for our piano keys,
Your feet for our stools.

Big grey elephant in the savannah,
Elephant, I heard you crying.

Elephant scared with a panic
Crying for your life,
Great elephant
You're dying.

Your tusks for our piano keys,
Your feet for our stools.

Giant grey elephant in the savannah,
Elephant, I heard you sobbing.

You make a sound like a trumpet
And you rumble and call.

I heard your heart,
It was fast and loud.

We would make you dumb.

Your tusks for our piano keys,
Your feet for our stools.

Hannah Patterson (8)
Oaklands School, Loughton

The Song Of The Tiger

Your fur coats for our cold bodies.
Your claws for my health.

Growling creature in the jungle
Tiger, I heard you sobbing.

Oh tiger, sobbing for your life
I know we would use your dying.

Your fur coats for our cold bodies.
Your claws for my health.

Roaring creature in the jungle
Tiger, I heard you crying.

Growling, hissing, roaring
Your heart beats like a thumping drum.

We would make you dumb.

Your fur coats for our cold bodies.
Your claws for my health.

Trinity Star Smith (9)
Oaklands School, Loughton

The London Eye

When I went up high in the sky,
It felt like my feet could fly.
My head spun round like a whist of wind,
I could almost see the world!
My eyes went all dizzy,
My water turned fizzy,
I just stood there and gazed.

When I went up high in the sky,
I nearly grew wings!
I jumped around and fluttered,
Up and down, up and down.
It felt so magical,
I wish I lived encased forever.
I just stood there and gazed.

When I went up high in the sky,
I had to fly back down again.
I went down slowly to take in the view.
If you're wondering where I was,
You can go there yourself too,
I went on the amazing London Eye.

Isabella Singer (10)
Oaklands School, Loughton

The Song Of The Tiger

Your fur coats to keep us warm
Your claws for our Chinese medicines

Roaring majestic animal in the jungle
Tiger, I heard you growling for your safety

Great tiger lying on the floor
Dreaming your last
Nobody can save you
You are dying

Your fur coats to keep us warm
Your claws for our Chinese medicines

Thunderous animal in the jungle
Tiger, I heard you growling in sadness

Growling, hissing, roaring
Your heart beating rapidly and thunderous
We made you dumb

Your fur coats to keep us warm
Your claws for our Chinese medicines.

Olivia Mor (9)
Oaklands School, Loughton

The Song Of The Elephant

Your feet as stools for our comfort
Your ivory for our ornaments.

Beautiful beast in the savannah
Elephant, I heard you crying
Crying for your life
I know how we use your dying.

Elegant beast in the savannah
Elephant, I heard you trumpeting
I can hear your heart beating rapidly.

We would make you dumb.

Your feet as stools for our comfort
Your ivory for our ornaments.

Charlotte Bastock (8)
Oaklands School, Loughton

The Song Of The Elephant

Your tusks for our jewellery
Your feet for our stools

Huge elegant beast
Thumping through the scrubland

Elephant, I hear you crying

Great elephant you're sulking for your kind
Crying for your kind

Your tusks for our jewellery
Your feet for our stools

I can hear your heartbeat
Like a toy drum

We would make you dumb

Your tusks for our jewellery
Your feet for our stools.

Gabriella Celentano (9)
Oaklands School, Loughton

The Song Of The Ape

Your hands for our ash trays,
Your babies for our pets.

A brown ball of wool in a rainforest, on the trees,
Ape I heard you weeping.

Great ape, weeping for your safety,
Weeping for your friends,
I know how we use your murder.

Your hands for our ash trays,
Your babies for our pets.

A big ball of wool in a rainforest,
Ape, I heard you disappointed.

Monkey calling, banging and scratching
When they swing it's a repetitive heartbeat.

We would make you dumb.

Your hands for our ash trays,
Your babies for our pets.

Brooke Hall (8)
Oaklands School, Loughton

The Song Of The Turtle

Your meat for our soup
Your eggs for our food

Huge creature in the sea
Turtle, I heard you crying

Great turtle sobbing for your life
Cruel to use you for us
Your death

Your meat for our soup
Your eggs for our food

Beautiful creature in the sea
Turtle, I heard you panicking

Crying, sobbing, whimpering

I heard your heart beating
Like thunder and lightning

We would make you dumb

Your meat for our soup
Your eggs for our food.

Amani Rashid (8)
Oaklands School, Loughton

Song Of The Rhino

Your horns for our medicines
Your horns for our Chinese strength
You live in the savannah
You are giant
You don't make a lot of noise
Rhino, I heard you panicking
Sad rhino you are panicking alone
Your horns for our medicines
Your horns for Chinese strength
You live in the beautiful, gigantic savannah
You are giant
You don't make a lot of noise
Rhino, I heard you panicking
The sounds of calling for help and crying
I hear your heart beating like thunder
We would make you dumb
Your horns for our medicines
Your horns for our Chinese strength.

Scarlett Citroen (8)
Oaklands School, Loughton

My Rainforest Poem

Peacefully
the butterfly hovered in the understorey.
Quickly
the snake slithered through the trees.
Immediately
the parrot flew to the kapok tree.
Cheekily
the monkeys swung from vine to vine.
Violently
the crocodile snapped his jaws.
Carefully
the leaves swished up in the canopy.

Ellie Cullen (8)
St Albans Catholic Primary School, Harlow

My Rainforest Poem

Cheekily
the monkey swung from tree to tree.
Carefully
the ladybird crawled on a bright green leaf.
Gently
the parrot flew through the clear blue sky.
Loudly
the lion roared to wake the lazy orang-utans.
Proudly
the snake slithered up the beautiful tree.
Lightly
the butterflies fluttered away from their nests.
Breezily
the trees swished from side to side.
Speedily
the tiger crept up on his prey.

Alice Humphreys (9)
St Albans Catholic Primary School, Harlow

Rainforest

Carefully
jaguars crept up trees.
Silently
snakes slid through the leaves.
Slowly
sloths swung from vines.
Gently
butterflies fluttered to the flowers.

Owen Wall (8)
St Albans Catholic Primary School, Harlow

My Rainforest Poem

Silently,
the tiger crept up on his prey.
Proudly,
the jaguar trod through the mysterious forest.
Slowly,
the snake slithered behind the giant kapok tree.
Carefully,
the toucan flew up, round and down the trees.
Quickly,
the butterfly hovered round the understorey.
Cleverly,
the orang-utan built his leafy umbrella.
Gently,
the trees waved in the cool breeze.
Cheekily,
the monkeys swung from tree to tree.
Lazily,
the sloth climbed the great kapok tree.
Curiously,
we leave the forest.

Eve Corcoran (9)
St Albans Catholic Primary School, Harlow

My Rainforest Poem

Silently, the butterfly fluttered her wings.
Quickly, the snake disappeared between the grass.
Slowly, the flower grew brightly.
Noisily, the rattlesnake slithered around the rainforest.
Cleverly, the monkey swung from the understorey to the canopy.
Viciously, the tiger ripped the feathers off a toucan.
Can we save the rainforest?
Will we?

Yedhu Karthikeyan (8)
St Albans Catholic Primary School, Harlow

My Rainforest Poem

Patiently,
the tiger crept up on his prey.
Lazily,
the sloth wandered around the tree.
Slowly,
the snake slithered behind the green grass.
Silently,
the butterfly hovered over the under story.
Quickly,
the huge tree fell down to the ground.
Cheekily,
the monkey threw his banana skin.
Noisily,
the parrot squawked at the top of the canopy.

Euan Reynolds (8)
St Albans Catholic Primary School, Harlow

My Rainforest Poem

Quietly,
the tiger climbed the lovely trees.
Proudly,
the sloth walked happily through the rainforest.
Slowly,
the snake slithered under the understorey.
Gently,
the monkey swung through the trees.
Angrily,
the gorilla rushed through the forest.
Loudly,
the crocodile snapped.

Liam Dunlea (8)
St Albans Catholic Primary School, Harlow

The Beautiful Rainforest

The beautiful rainforest, the beautiful rainforest,
Where many creatures live
Like the Alexandra birdwing - *flutter, flutter, flutter*
And the three-toed sloth climbing up the trees
And wiggling his knees
The jaguars roaring while the parrots are squawking
Everything prancing, everything dancing,
Where snakes slither and slide
And the crocs snap and glide
As the moon comes up, the animals drink from the watering hole cup

The beautiful rainforest, the beautiful rainforest
As far as the eye can see
The beautiful rainforest, the beautiful rainforest
Is endangered by you and me
The wild yak, the Andean mountain cat are struggling to survive
The corroboree frog, the African wild dog are fighting to stay alive

The beautiful rainforest, the beautiful rainforest, help us please
To stop the men cutting down our trees
The world is a big place and it's plain to see,
That without greed, we all can live in harmony
Save the rainforest for you and me.

Emma Martini (9)
St Albans Catholic Primary School, Harlow

My Rainforest Poem

Carefully a jaguar crept through the grass.
Silently a snake slithered up a tree.
Slowly a sloth swung and swung.
Gently a butterfly fluttered.
Proudly a toucan flies and flies.
Hardly trees blow about.
Slowly a monkey swings from branch to branch.

Jessica Payne (8)
St Albans Catholic Primary School, Harlow

My Rainforest Poem

Proudly,
the toucan flew through the trees.
Loudly,
the parrot squawked from high up in the canopy.
Carefully,
the sloth climbed slowly not to fall.
Silently,
the snake slithered slowly across the ground.
Happily,
the story ends.

Matthew Barry (8)
St Albans Catholic Primary School, Harlow

My Rainforest Poem

Slowly
the sloth was smiling.
Quickly
the cheeky monkeys swung from tree to tree.
Immediately
the gorillas both ran with each other.
Excitedly
the parrots were flying above the canopy.
Cleverly
the cheetah jumped to get his prey.
Slowly
the butterfly was hovering in the understorey.
Slowly
the tiger opened his mouth.
Silently
the snake slithered up the wooden tree.
Slowly
the crocodile opened his mouth.

Jessica Marsham (8)
St Albans Catholic Primary School, Harlow

My Rainforest Poem

Carefully,
the jaguar crept up on his prey.
Silently,
the snake slithered up a tree.
Slowly,
a sloth swung along the trees.
Gently,
a butterfly fluttered through the grass.
Proudly,
a monkey swung from tree to tree.
Quietly,
the story ends.

Ellen Barrett (8)
St Albans Catholic Primary School, Harlow

My Rainforest Poem

Carefully the jaguar crept quietly across the rocky stones.
Silently the sloth clambered up the tall tree.
Slowly the snake slithered through the rough grass.
Loudly the tiger roared at the monkeys.
Peacefully the butterfly fluttered through the under story.
Quickly the chimpanzee swung through the trees stealing bananas.
Cheekily the monkey stole a banana.
Calmly the orangutan bit the crunchy leaves.
Gently the parrot squawked in the sky.
Rapidly the toucan roamed in the sky.
Amazingly the toad slithered through the mud.

Dylan Andrew (9)
St Albans Catholic Primary School, Harlow

My Rainforest

Carefully, the jaguar crept nervously.
Silently, the snake slithered carefully.
Slowly, the trees swished.
Gently, the cheeky monkey swung.
Proudly, the Venus flytrap snapped with happiness.
Croakily, the frogs hiccupped on their lily pads.
Noisily, the parrots squawked from high up in the canopy.

Sean Smith (8)
St Albans Catholic Primary School, Harlow

My Rainforest Poem

Gently,
the leaves waved.
Fiercely,
the lion roared.
Cheekily,
the orang-utan jumped away from the cheetah.
Quickly,
the parrots squawked.
Slowly,
the slug crept away.
Loudly,
the cheetah crept on its prey.
Immediately,
the sloth walked across the branches.

Tom Pryor (9)
St Albans Catholic Primary School, Harlow

Rainforest Poem

Slowly Jake the snake slithered into the lake.
Patiently the tiger pounced at its prey.
The maddest monkey swung from branch to branch.
Loudly the parrot squawked from the top of the canopy.
Angrily the gorilla marched through the trees.
Calmly we leave the forest.

Jasmine Attridge (9)
St Albans Catholic Primary School, Harlow

My Rainforest Poem

Carefully,
the monkey swung from branch to branch.
Slowly,
the tiger yawned in the long grass.
Loudly,
the crocodile snapped at his prey.
Cleverly,
the small tiger crept up on his prey.

Fraser Cochrane (9)
St Albans Catholic Primary School, Harlow

My Rainforest Poem

Carefully,
the big sloth slid down from the wide tree.
Silently,
the massive tiger killed the deer.
Quickly,
the jaguar climbed the big tree.

Alex Baldwin (9)
St Albans Catholic Primary School, Harlow

My Rainforest Poem

Slowly,
the sloth crawled up the tree.
Immediately,
the tiger pounced on his prey.
Cheekily,
the monkey swung through the trees.
Lightly,
the frog croaked, jumping from branch to branch.
Loudly,
the toucan squawked in the canopy.
Meanly,
the lion ate his prey.
Quietly,
the rainforest goes to sleep again.

Solenne Boyce (8)
St Albans Catholic Primary School, Harlow

My Rainforest Poem

Slowly
the green leaves waved.
Happily
the orang-utans silently climbed the trees.
Gently
the gloomy snakes slithered across the ground.
Fiercely
the scary lions roared.
Cheekily
the noisy monkeys swung from branch to branch.

Oliver Hufton (8)
St Albans Catholic Primary School, Harlow

My Rainforest Poem

Mischievously,
the snake slithered into the great kapok tree.
Furiously,
the monkey dashed through the long vines.
Elegantly,
the butterfly hovered into the trees.
Loudly,
the parrot squawked high up in the canopy.
Rudely,
the lion pounced through the understorey.

Nicole Fisher (9)
St Albans Catholic Primary School, Harlow

My Rainforest Poem

Slowly,
the sloth climbed up to the top of the tree.
Quickly,
the snakes slithered through the lush green grass.
Gently,
the monkey swung from branch to branch.
Cheekily,
tigers jumped to their babies.
Loudly,
the crocodiles snapped their mouths.
Quickly,
parrots spoke to each other.
Carefully,
the jaguars crept to their prey.

Sophie Ferran (9)
St Albans Catholic Primary School, Harlow

The Rainforest

Slowly,
the sloth climbed the waving trees.
Cheekily,
the monkeys swung from tree to tree.
Loudly,
the giant tiger roared.
Angrily,
the crazy gorilla rushed through the beautiful rainforest.
Silently,
the snake slithered.
Gently,
the leaves waved slowly.

Jake Dickson (8)
St Albans Catholic Primary School, Harlow

My Rainforest Poem

Carefully
Jaguar crept through the tree.
Silently
Snake slithered through the grass.
Slowly
The sloth swung lazily.
Gently
The frog jumped to get the fly.

Cavan Dixon (8)
St Albans Catholic Primary School, Harlow

What Is . . . The Snow?

The snow is a fluffy white blanket,
All comfy and cosy.

It is like a leaf,
Swiftly falling from the sky.

It is as white as a white cloud,
On a hot summer's day.

It is like a fluffy coat,
That you wear around you.

Alex Sheridan-Brown (10)
St Andrew's CE Primary School, Soham

The Snow

Snow white crushing under your feet,
Snow glitters like a star in the dark night sky,
Gently it falls onto the ground,
Blanket children playing all wrapped up,
Snow, snow . . . we want more.

Natasha Shorney (9)
St Andrew's CE Primary School, Soham

What Is The Moon?

The moon is a silver coin,
Tossed into the sky.

It is a huge white world,
On a black chalkboard.

It is a fingerprint,
On a black piece of card.

It is the sun,
Turned into white instead of yellow.

Jack Swindlehurst (10)
St Andrew's CE Primary School, Soham

What Is . . . The Star?

A star is very shiny,
Then it's up in the sky.

It is a white beach star,
Next to a dark blue sea.

Star is shiny
As a light in a black room.

Dovydas Morkys (9)
St Andrew's CE Primary School, Soham

What Is . . . The Moon?

The moon is a glistening pearl
in my mum's jewellery box.
It is a shiny silver coin
left in darkness until morning.
It is an elegant swan
swimming over its reflection in the night sky.
The moon is like a special star
that twinkles in the night.

Joshua Riley (10)
St Andrew's CE Primary School, Soham

What Is . . . A Raindrop?

A raindrop is a tear,
Shed from Heaven.

It is a crystal jewel,
Lost from an elegant necklace.

It is a shard of glass,
Lost from a broken window.

Fiona Darlow (10)
St Andrew's CE Primary School, Soham

Snow

Snow . . . slowly falls to the ground.
It glitters in the early morning.
It is as white as a clean sheet of paper.
It gently lands on the ground waiting to melt.
It sounds like broken glass when you step on it.

Hannah de Oliveira Lloyd (10)
St Andrew's CE Primary School, Soham

Rainbow Fish

Scales rough . . . rough rock,
Sparkled like a pot of gold,
Stand out in glory.

Laney Gill (9)
St Andrew's CE Primary School, Soham

What Is The Snow?

The snow is a white blanket that fell to the ground.
It's an ice ring that the children play in.
The snow is like a cloud that fell to the ground.
The snow is like a moon fallen to the ground.
It's a crystal that has been smashed into pieces.

Morwenna Woodbridge (9)
St Andrew's CE Primary School, Soham

Snow

Snow . . . glimmers like a star in the sky.
Softly floating like an autumn leaf.
When it falls it makes a blanket.
It sparkles like glitter on a Christmas card.
Snow, as soft as cotton wool.
It is as shiny as a clear crystal.

Rubi Peachey (10)
St Andrew's CE Primary School, Soham

What Is . . . A Snowflake?

It is like a white marble bean
dropped from the heavens.

It is like a shiny bit of paper
fallen from the sky.

Quietly, softly . . . it's down,
like a banner drifting side to side.

Kayleigh Tofts (10)
St Andrew's CE Primary School, Soham

The Unicorn - Haiku

White as fresh laid snow,
Beautiful and very strong,
Gentle as a dove.

Lexie Ronketti (9)
St Andrew's CE Primary School, Soham

What Is . . . The Rainbow?

The rainbow is a colourful parrot,
talks to you like a best friend.

It is a shooting star,
that spreads across the sky.

It is a magical tunnel,
that will lead you to anywhere.

It is a colourful ocean
that lives in the sky.

It is the most beautiful sunset
you will ever see.

Juliana Crook (9)
St Andrew's CE Primary School, Soham

What Is . . . A Rainbow?

A rainbow is Joseph's coat
suspended in the sky.

It is a bridge,
carrying angels up to Heaven.

It is a colourful train track,
carrying trains over the calm sea.

It is a parachute,
floating down to Earth.

It is rays of paint,
flicked from a magical paintbrush.

Joseph de Oliveira Lloyd (10)
St Andrew's CE Primary School, Soham

What Is . . . A Snowflake?

A snowflake is a diamond
on a white pillow.

It is a frozen teardrop
from the heavens.

It is a white marble
dropped onto a white blanket.

It is white bonbons
being dropped into whipped cream.

Clarisse Allman (9)
St Andrew's CE Primary School, Soham

What Is . . . The Snow?

The snow is a white polar bear lying on the ice.
Snow is the moonlight in the midnight sky.
Snow is white glitter falling from the sky.
The snow is a white piece of paper.
Snow is sugar falling all around.
The snow is white feathers falling to the ground.
Snow is white nail polish shining in the sun.

Kacey Day (9)
St Andrew's CE Primary School, Soham

What Is . . . Snow?

It is like a blanket of snow
covering the floor.
It is like glitter
being sprinkled on the road.
It is like white glittering stars
falling from the sky.
It is like a polar bear
wearing a white woolly coat.

Charlie Fitt (9)
St Andrew's CE Primary School, Soham

What Is . . . A Rainbow?

A rainbow is colourful
like the sunset.
A rainbow is like a person
has kicked a beach ball in the air.
It's like an artist
has painted the sky in the night.
A rainbow is as colourful
as the flowers together in a vase.

Sara Dunbavin-Cox (10)
St Andrew's CE Primary School, Soham

Unicorn - Haiku

Graceful as a swan,
As powerful as a wave,
Flies away up high.

Rita Rodrigues (9)
St Andrew's CE Primary School, Soham

Horse - Haiku

They scuttle through fields,
Glamorous as a model,
They are fun to ride.

Olivia Avis (10)
St Andrew's CE Primary School, Soham

What Is . . . The Moon?

The moon is a ball of ice,
Inside a dark, dark fridge.

It is a football,
Kicked high into the sky.

It is a light bulb,
On a never-ending ceiling.

It is a bouncy ball,
Bounced into the void.

It is a skull,
Floating up to Heaven.

Tom Humbles (9)
St Andrew's CE Primary School, Soham

Eagle - Haiku

Stalks its victim . . . strikes,
Dive bombs on prey at high speeds,
Amazing to see.

Owen Lupton-Pike (9)
St Andrew's CE Primary School, Soham

Snowmen

S nowmen melting in the sun,
N o looking back at the snow,
O h, another day has come,
W hatever happens on each day,
M en build snowmen in the snow,
E ven though they are men,
N o one can stop the sun.

Amy Conway (10)
St Cedd's CE Primary School, Bradwell on Sea

Jealousy

The courtyard was a boggy lake of leaves crackling in the misty air
The stable was an abandoned tree house with ivy racing through the cracks
The house was a rubbish dump with barely a piece of wood as support
And as the fog covered everything visible, two ghostly figures emerged.

Her hair was spilt red wine shining in the moonlight
Her eyes were diamonds sparkling brighter than the stars
Her lips were fluffy marshmallows, covered rose pink
And as she kissed her true love, she drifted into Heaven.

The naked horse chestnut tree leaned closer to the ground
A tawny owl sent its calling as it flew out of sight
A colony of vampire bats awakened from their sleep
And as the clock struck midnight a ghastly silhouette appeared

His hair was burnt toast crumbling in the gusty breeze
His eyes were tunnels of foolishness, burrowing through his mind
His lips, charcoal dust smudged over every corner
And as he heard the laughing, he took the dagger from his pocket . . .

Alice Jeary (11)
St Cedd's CE Primary School, Bradwell on Sea

Scary Man

Scary man, scary man, cutting down a tree
Scary man, scary man, coming to kill me
Scary man, scary man, gone to prison
Scary man, scary man, learning about triangular prisms.

Grace Bentley (11)
St Cedd's CE Primary School, Bradwell on Sea

Ellie The Dog

Ellie the dog is as cute as can be,
She got all excited when she saw my sisters and me.
She's small as a baby and brown as a bear,
Her fur is all curly, just like my sister's hair.

We went to the seaside, and this is where we played.
She jumped like a bunny, and ran like a hare.
We could not catch her, so we just watched and stared.

She was very boisterous, like a child at a party.
She licked at our faces, like a child licking a lolly
Mummy was laughing but Amy didn't think it was so funny.
Ellie the dog is as cute as can be!

Chloe Stratton (10)
St Cedd's CE Primary School, Bradwell on Sea

Fire

I enjoy making flaring fires
Because to make a fire is my best desire
They bang, crackle and snap in flames
I poke the fire with long pointy canes
As you look into the flames Hell rises up
The Devil himself bloodthirsty he drinks from his cup
The smoke curls and spirals all around
Because the fire is on the wet ground
I like orange, reds and yellows
But what's better than toasting marshmallows.

Andrew Hart (11)
St Cedd's CE Primary School, Bradwell on Sea

The Predator

He strikes his prey with blades of fury and blood.
He leaps place to place like a kangaroo in monster form.
Heat ray vision, X-ray vision,
He cycles through different visions for different enemies.
The ability to camouflage to any object like a chameleon.
A ninja he is like, he hunts his prey well.
All we know he's it's called The Predator!

Conner Livermore (11)
St Cedd's CE Primary School, Bradwell on Sea

This Morning I Saw The Classroom

This morning I saw the classroom quiet
Tables messy, pencils scattered on the messy tables
Teachers get bored of the quietness
Children burst through the door with excitement
But children get bored of helping the teachers.

This morning I saw the classroom
Dirty classrooms become tidy, shiny as can be
Leaky taps turned off by children
Quiet fire bells dangle from walls
Children leave the room for break
Teachers left alone again.

This morning I saw the classroom
Teachers get the children from the dirty playground
Children burst the door open to go home
All staff go home without headaches.

Hope Brooks (11)
St James' CE (VA) Primary School, Colchester

This Morning I Saw The Classroom . . .

This morning I saw the classroom waiting
Blistering sunlight as hot as a desert
Tables like shiny ice rinks with the stage and elegant dancer on top
Needle sharp pencils waiting to be used by eager children.

This morning I saw the classroom chuckling
Anthologies talking to the pupil books
Scissors cutting to their destination
Sticky PVA glue staining like a huge blob of snow.

This morning I saw the quiet classroom counting
Numbers 1-100, boasting because they are the most immense
numbers of all
The add and take away sign are playing a mathematical game.

This morning I saw the classroom sitting down
Chair legs settling down on the floor
Glistening tables stretching as far as an eye can see
Shelves growing bigger and bigger.

This morning I saw the classroom flying
Whiteboards hung up high on the walls
Water cycle posters seeking up high
Times tables climbing to the top of Mount Cupboard.

This morning I saw the classroom spring to life
Doors opening like book pages, windows open for a fresh start
And school gates burst open as the torrent of children comes gushing in.

Ryan Norfolk (9)
St James' CE (VA) Primary School, Colchester

This Morning I Saw The Classroom

This morning I saw the quiet classroom,
Children being silent in the classroom,
Inky black pen, multicoloured pencils writing on plain white paper,
Loud, annoying children and teachers becoming bored.

This late morning I saw the worrying classroom,
Because no children were coming,
Boring teachers weren't there, they were in bed,
Sharp pencils standing in their yellow pots.

This morning I saw the crying classroom,
Teachers staring at the green, round globe,
Children asking the teachers, 'What are you staring at?'

Chloe Penn Bowen (11)
St James' CE (VA) Primary School, Colchester

This Morning I Saw The Classroom

This morning I saw the classroom waiting,
The colourful bell went off and I knew the lovely peace was fading away.
As the wild children grabbed their pencils and go to work
The shimmering, shining sun turned to deathly dark doom.

This morning I saw the annoying children sighing,
Work on walls getting creased,
Curled and cut as kids fiddle with it every minute of the dusty, dark days.

This morning I saw the lovely, clean, tidy tables turn really mucky
After the children have stuck sticky, squishy bubblegum under their desks,
Spilt white clouds of glue everywhere.
At least it's home time.

Jemma Hewes (10)
St James' CE (VA) Primary School, Colchester

This Morning I Saw The Classroom . . .

Early this morning I saw the empty classroom
impatiently waiting, dusty desks
and brilliant work on walls,
leftover pencil cases and the teacher's desk untidy,
looking like a mountain of rubbish.

This morning I saw the classroom
dancing, rubber bands drifting through the air
like crows on an excellent day,
tables moonwalking left and right,
small rubbers bouncing all over the place
like pogo sticks.

This morning I saw the classroom
chattering with coldness, the door wide open
like a baby wanting a hug,
boys chewing Extra mint gum
which makes their breath cold.

This morning I saw the classroom
vibrating, the teacher's nerve twitching
whilst waiting for her class
as if they were a loading computer,
pencils dropping on the floor
making it shatter.

This morning I saw the classroom
scribbling, pencils skating across the ice colour paper,
permanent markers moving left and right on the whiteboard.

Jordan Wiltsher (9)
St James' CE (VA) Primary School, Colchester

This Morning I Saw The Classroom

This morning I saw the classroom empty.
Great gusts of people faking the flu
While eating some stew.

This morning I saw the classroom exploding.
Lots of people shouting in silent reading
While terrified teachers are dying.

This morning I saw the classroom crying.
Razor sharp scissors cutting old ancient dictionaries
And huge blunt pencils over exceptional books.

Adnan Hussain (10)
St James' CE (VA) Primary School, Colchester

This Morning I Saw The Classroom

This morning I see the classroom empty and quiet
So the annoying sounds of the fire alarm went off.
As the annoying sounds went off
The naughty children rushed in squishing and pushing.

This morning I observed the classroom filled with smoke.
It was burning toast in the toaster.

This morning I recognise the classroom's noisy teachers
Rushing in while leaving the children behind.
'Hopefully they knew we forgot them,' said the teachers.

This morning I spot the classroom so dramatic
Even some of the girls started crying
Because of the fire alarm they thought it was a real fire.

This morning I witness the classroom at yummy lunch time.
All the girls eat poshly and the boys munch and crunch their food.

This morning I see the classroom quiet.
After a while the fire alarm turned off and we went inside.

Leia Rudge (9)
St James' CE (VA) Primary School, Colchester

This Morning I Found The Classroom Silent

This morning I found the classroom silent,
Chairs standing still and silent on tables,
Pencils everywhere,
On the floor, tables and chairs,
Everything quiet.

This morning I found the classroom bursting with noise,
Children scraping chairs on the floor,
Piercing noise as people pushed tables back and forth,
Hurting themselves whilst they did it.

This morning I found the classroom fidgeting,
Children fiddling with their normal but blunt writing pencils,
Rubbers and pencil cases as well,
Silence hit the classroom,
All you could hear was the screeching whiteboard pen,
As if it was a screeching mouse.

This morning I found the classroom deafening,
Children bellowing across the littered classroom,
Gossiping with their friends,
Roaring like a thousand lions including the stressed teacher,
Some people throwing objects around.

This morning I found the classroom silent,
Children doing their work,
All you could hear was the scraping of pencils,
The odd noise of people fidgeting.

This morning I found the classroom ear-splitting,
Children pulling their chairs across the clean floor,
Moving the cold seats around,
Everyone chatting to each other,
The head teacher trying to get them all quiet,
Annoyed class teacher gets them to work in silence.

Serena Campbell (10)
St James' CE (VA) Primary School, Colchester

This Morning I Saw The Classroom

This morning I saw the classroom empty,
Tables reflecting the bright light,
Pencils like knives, standing as straight as soldiers,
Blue jumpers all creased on the dirty chairs.

This morning I saw the children rushing in,
Coats and bags thrown everywhere,
Sharp pencils dancing elegantly across the clear page,
Rubbers flying through the air.

This morning I saw the classroom full,
A cool child slouching in the corner with a dunce hat on,
Unwashed paint pallets stacked as tall as the teacher,
Dusty books on the shelf waiting to be used.

This morning I saw the classroom getting bored,
Teachers jabbering on,
Striped pencils scattered everywhere,
Raining dust from the blackboard,
Excellent work falling off the filthy walls.

This afternoon I saw the stuffy classroom,
Children reading their dusty books,
The finger was skating on the ripped pages,
The teachers were stressed more than ever.

The clock was ticking and tocking!
The bell rang and shook all the dust off,
It was the end of the day!

Ellie-May Griggs (9)
St James' CE (VA) Primary School, Colchester

This Morning I See The Classroom

This morning I see the tiresome classroom waiting.
Tables like ice rinks glisten and gleam,
Waiting for pencil cases to skate for hours and hours.
The clear timetable waiting for the fingers to slide and slide
All over and finally being used
And the plain clock ticking, *tick-tock!*

This morning I see the frustrated classroom shouting.
Fidgeting children tapping their ruined pencils on the tables,
Getting the calm teacher into a stressed teacher
Caring friends having fake fights and screaming their heads off
And the clean whiteboard turning filthy
All because of the squeaky pen dancing carelessly across.

This morning I see the abandoned classroom crying.
English books weeping their words out as sadly they're unmarked.
Unsharpened pencils rolling all over the place
As they didn't have any heads,
And the toilet book crying its eyes out as it was empty and unused.

This morning I see the drowsy classroom yawning.
The huge map convincing all the countries to sleep,
And the pupils' gratifying work falls asleep
And doesn't realise it's stuck in an island of gloopy glue.

Maria Jaskula (9)
St James' CE (VA) Primary School, Colchester

This Morning I Saw The Classroom . . .

This morning I saw the classroom waking up,
As I sat there waiting for the class to come bursting in.
I was waiting for pencils to be dancing across paper.

This morning I saw the classroom shining,
I could see the dust, the sunlight dancing around
As I turned on the heater.

This morning I saw children bursting into the classroom,
Screaming with laughter as the sticky glue pot went over.
'It looks like an island!' the children said.
This morning I saw children,
The lunch hall starving for hungry children.

Neve Cornwell (10)
St James' CE (VA) Primary School, Colchester

This Lazy Morning

This lazy morning
I saw my friends spilling some glue like a big blob of snow
Bits of coloured pencils' lead on the shining floor
And teachers slipping on banana skins.

School is boring!

This morning I saw the boring old classroom
With a wet floor sign on the floor
Lots of tennis balls being brought in from the playground
And muddy Liverpool kits in the dirty wet cloakroom.

This morning just before English
I saw pencils dancing the conga
Squeaking old pens on the ancient whiteboard
And toddlers crying to their mums,
'I don't want to go to nursery.'

This morning I saw people playing catch indoors
Silly clowns getting dragged across the room
And children thinking that their pencils are cigarettes.

Christopher Carnaffin (9)
St James' CE (VA) Primary School, Colchester

This Morning I Saw The Classroom

This morning I saw the classroom empty,
As quiet as a ladybird,
As I slowly strolled around the empty classroom,
I had a quick look at all the displays.

This morning I saw the classroom deserted,
It was the first time it was that quiet,
It felt so strange because it was abandoned.

This morning I saw the classroom silent,
Tables glisten like burnished ice rinks,
English books ready for the children to write in.

This morning I saw the classroom chattering,
A great sudden chatter filled the classroom,
The chairs suddenly banging,
The trays rattling.

This afternoon I saw the classroom hungry,
Great gusts of peckish children lining up for lunch,
Hungry youngsters sitting at the table.

This afternoon I saw the classroom empty,
All the presentations that the children have done shiny and excellent,
As quiet as a spider.

Muminah Miah (9)
St James' CE (VA) Primary School, Colchester

This Morning In The Classroom

This morning, I saw the classroom full,
Children getting bored while doing impossible work.
Children stuck and some desperately needed the toilet.

This morning in the classroom
Forceful teachers telling kids what to do.
The resounding fire bell goes off.
Kids lining up in panic to go outside.

In the cold classroom
I saw people looking out of the dirty window
At the glistening white snow.

In the sparkling classroom
I saw pitch black cupboards with stuffed folders inside.
An adventuristic parachutist landing outside.

Kyle Wordsworth (10)
St James' CE (VA) Primary School, Colchester

This Morning I Saw The Classroom

This morning I saw the classroom awaking
For a whole new day,
Children fidgeting and fiddling,
All the tables glistening and impatient,
Rubbers skating across the table.

This morning I saw the classroom waiting
For children to do their English
Children were making a mess
With the new writing pens
After that the children were tidying up.

This morning I saw the classroom
My PE bag walking along to the classroom
Because it wanted to get in the PE box.
After noon I finished my last lesson
The clock said it was home time.

Chloe Hinson (9)
St James' CE (VA) Primary School, Colchester

This Morning I Saw The Classroom

This morning I saw the classroom rushing.
Tables are sparkling like diamonds,
Pencils stand pointed in the pencil pots,
At the classroom I saw the children
Making the books skate on the tables.

This morning I saw the classroom singing,
Dancing, playing piano and playing drums,
Workings on the walls looks great.

This morning I saw the children
Making the classrooms gorgeous,
The children of the classroom
Are sitting very nicely to go for lunch.

This afternoon I saw children eating their food,
The school dinners making noise.

This afternoon I saw the children
Messing up their classroom and playing games.

This afternoon I saw the children
Sitting very nicely listening to the story that the teacher says.

This afternoon I saw the children
Making the classroom beautiful again.

Reeja Mary Rajan (9)
St James' CE (VA) Primary School, Colchester

This Morning Outside The Classroom

This morning outside the classroom
I was waiting and it was so quiet
I could even hear the clock ticking
It even felt like it was laughing at me
Because I was in the rain.

This morning it went from quiet to loud
As the bell went and children burst in
And teachers became strict
For the rest of the day.

In the classroom eager children wanted to learn
But next door was shouting and banging
Rulers put their hands on their ears
And jumped into their children's trays.

Harry Gardner (9)
St James' CE (VA) Primary School, Colchester

This Morning I Saw The Classroom

This morning I saw the classroom empty
And quiet as can be.
While the stressed teacher marked boring math books
While sipping his scorching tea.

This morning I saw the classroom getting as ready as can be
To let the naughty children in.
Then with a thud an explosion of children
Came through the door.

This morning I saw the dinner hall watching young children
As they went in slowly and raced out to play.
Meanwhile the juniors were starting to eat hot dogs,
Curly fries and baked beans.

Bethany Jennings (9)
St James' CE (VA) Primary School, Colchester

This Morning I Saw The Classroom

This morning I saw the classroom
Water from the tap goes *drip drop*
Wanting to be an ocean going *whoosh.*

This morning when the children came in
It was like they had never seen a classroom before,
Shouting so loud, I could hardly think.

This morning in history we were learning about World War II,
The noise of the bombs exploding
Making me feel terrified!

This morning I heard the low rumbling of the children's stomachs
Like thunder going far away
Lunch time!

Adam Smith (9)
St James' CE (VA) Primary School, Colchester

This Morning

This morning I saw the classroom getting very grumpy,
They moan when they do lame Egyptian work
And get greedy off playing a simple game of chess
Then go in the edge of the room and lurk.

This morning I saw the classroom being lazy,
Not cleaning the room and throwing pencils under the table,
Asking for rubbers instead of getting one.

This morning I saw the classroom getting bored.
Everything standing quiet and moaning,
When they wanted lots of toys but they had to do lame work.

This morning I saw the classroom reading,
Some read loud and some read quietly
And some books read with good expression
And some read in their books with their neat pension.

Kyle Tibudan (9)
St James' CE (VA) Primary School, Colchester

This Morning I Saw The Classroom

This morning I heard the quiet drip of the waterfall
To the bottom of the sink and the fresh smell of a clean classroom.
The scary teacher was using a table as a mirror
While kids tumbled into their boring school ready to work.

This morning I heard the fire alarm
Overjoyed that the caretaker made it ring for a fire drill.
The teacher was shouting because of the glue island
Surrounding the table.

At playtime I got beaten up, big fists shot at my eyes,
The teacher does nothing,
I'm not one of the teacher's favourites.

This morning I saw the classroom
My best friend left school, no one cares
I have no other friends.
Before he left he gave me a poem.
It read: 'I have a new home in Rome
Please take care of my fish in the dome
Put the dome on some foam'.

Joshua Harrington (8)
St James' CE (VA) Primary School, Colchester

I Am Autumn

I am Autumn.
My cloak is the bright blue sky,
My smile is the beams of sunlight,
The leaves run through the shivering grass,
My chilled tears are the crisp falling leaves,
My breath is the silky clouds
Which are like beautiful new ribbons floating in the sky,
My eyes are the jewels in the frost,
I am Autumn.

Eleanor Rose Aitchison (11)
St James' RC Primary School, Orpington

Autumn

The morning dew is my icy tears.
The breeze is my breath,
Steaming up any glass in its path.
Swaying in the breeze,
The trees are my bare arms.
The crispy autumn leaves rustling,
Every time pounded on by a foot is my voice.
The birds chirping loud,
Is me bellowing like a foghorn in the night.
My gaze is the sunlight flickering through the trees.

David Ambrose (11)
St James' RC Primary School, Orpington

Snow

Snow is gentle,

Delighting mortals all around,
Covering the barren ground,
Watching all the children's faces,
As they have great sledging races.

But,
Snow can be merciless.

Wreaking havoc everywhere,
Making people stop and stare,
Confining all to their room,
Stopping life in great gloom.

When snow is gentle,
Life seems great,
When snow is merciless,
Our only memories are hate.

Some like the snow,
Some want it to go,
But it'll always be here,
So let's bring it on with a cheer!

Kate Benson (10)
St James' RC Primary School, Orpington

Christmas Is Coming

Christmas is coming, I can't wait
Presents, puddings, turkey on the plate

Christmas presents, hard to find
Get them chocolate, they won't mind

Family all around, laughter everywhere
Joyous times, filling the air

Pulling the crackers, sharing a joke
Filling up our bellies, with snacks and Coke

The children open their presents at the start of dawn
But let's not forget it's about Jesus being born

Everyone round the table, not a sad face anywhere
But before we cut the turkey, let's say a prayer.

Angelica Davis (10)
St James' RC Primary School, Orpington

My Goldfish

Round and round I go all day,
In-between coral and castles I make my way.
I swim and I swim between morning and night,
The crab at the bottom gives me a good fright.
It's hard swimming first left then right,
Then back to the start to make sure I'm doing it right.
I am a goldfish, not quite a whale,
I'm a bit smaller when drawn to scale.
A short span of attention just like my master,
When he is doing maths it's quite a disaster!
Happy I go round in my bowl,
It's better than living down in a hole!

Rory Forde (11)
St James' RC Primary School, Orpington

Wondering

Stars scattered carelessly, shimmering like silver tears,
Masking the endless blackness in a haze of glowing light.
Space dust dyes their lustre scarlet
Giddily I gaze into the sky
Wondering.

Planets rotating wearily, tired of their endless path,
Teasing each other half-heartedly, belittling the dwarves.
Saturn is the millionaire, dripping in golden rings.
Filled with wonder, I gaze into the sky
Wondering.

Asteroids soar in fashionable belts, a swagger in their glide,
Laughing as they dent their fellow space residents.
Showering pebbles in their wake, the asteroids dive,
Dazed, I gaze into the sky
Wondering.

Satellites circle our planet, constantly beaming and scrambling.
Lost in nothingness, broken down, the objects sway
And lunge almost idly.
Oblivious to our appreciation, the satellites rasp
Overcome, I gaze into the sky
Wondering.

Black holes snarl and leer, beckoning us to their clutches.
Pleasure taken in every kill, the vortexes glare,
Time-blackened teeth grind expectantly, waiting for their refreshment.
Staggered, I gaze into the sky
Wondering.

The sun, a blazing ball of fury, writhes and thrashes in our midst.
A gingered orb elevated above us glows,
Feeling bashful in winter and brazen in summer.
She hides at dusk, reappearing at dawn, slumbering below the horizon.
Speechless, I gaze into the sky
Wondering.

The endless bounds of eternity, home to Earth our residence.
Telescopes scan a millionth of the sky, all we shall ever see from home.
Space's ancient secrets will never be told,
Astounded I gaze into the sky
Wondering . . .

Olivia Dean (11)
St James' RC Primary School, Orpington

Fulham Football Club

Fulham Football Club,
A wonderful place to be,
And if you don't believe me,
Then come along and see.

Craven Cottage is where we play,
That's where you'll find me on a Saturday,
Keeping warm with a cup of tea,
Thirty thousand fans and me.

Mark Hughes is the manager for us,
A great player, in his time, he was,
With squad players Davies, Elm and Duff,
We hope this season we'll have done enough.

We don't always win,
It's a bit of a shame,
But at the end of the day,
It's been a good game.

When I think where we've come from,
It's been a great ride,
If you want to join me,
Then stick by my side.

Thomas Deasy (11)
St James' RC Primary School, Orpington

School Days

When I get up I am forced out of bed
I get dressed and get myself fed
I leave in a hurry
On my way to school I have to scurry
It's loud in the playground
Hard to listen
It changes when I am in class
Not a noise, not even a whistle
We read and write and watch a sight
When the teacher shouts she is quite a fright

We learn to spell
Which we do quite well
Maths is the hardest
Sometimes the children have a problem to solve
And they don't know how
And when they get it right the teacher says, 'Wow!'

We do a few tests
The silence is frightening
And when we get the results back
The relief is amazing

Lunch is the best time
The children are excited
And when they taste that chocolate cake
The children are delighted

When the end of the day comes
The children are insane
It's not long before they realise they have to come back
Tomorrow and do it all again!

Olivia Elms-Lester (10)
St James' RC Primary School, Orpington

Autumn

The autumn moon is her gloomy chariot,
lowly and slowly.

Fallen twigs are her oily strands of hair,
crackling underfoot.

Autumn winds are her expostulations with spring,
never ceasing.

The rough, coarse bark is her tanned skin,
firm and strong.

Butterflies are her bewildering brooches,
trapped to her cloak, alive.

Glassy dewdrops are her tears,
shimmering and glimmering like golden dust.

Blackbird, autumn's spy, searches the dismal Earth for happiness
. . . draining all its sources.

Then, light fades, the sun dies, snow falls,
Autumn is no longer seen.

Daniel Ilsley (11)
St James' RC Primary School, Orpington

Snow

The crystal sands cover the land but not on the sunny beaches.
It lies quite still around my heels but crunches when I walk.
Time has stopped, nothing popped not even the wind could blow.
It's cold out here so keep your jacket near but don't stay long
Or you might catch the flu.
Soft and cold, new and old there's always something about it.
It's always white but never bright like yellow, orange or pink.
Falling down from the sky so high it gently strokes your face.
There's nothing to see so go back and have tea
Or you might as well watch the snow.

Simona Iorio (10)
St James' RC Primary School, Orpington

The Haunted House

I am the figure who watches
Waiting
Watches as you open the creaking door
I slam it behind you
Watches when you look around the cobweb-covered room
I make the moans and groans you hear
Watches when you climb the crumbling staircase
I blow the cold breeze you shiver upon feeling
Watches when you scour the boarded windows
I am the one who makes the faint crack of wood splitting
Revealing myself just when you think you are safely out the door
For I am your imagination.

Helena Mather (11)
St James' RC Primary School, Orpington

The Sense Of Autumn

Wispy leaves abseil down the thick trees
when the wind talks.

Drips fly down damp benches
and squeak on the shoe leather.

Spiders stitch twigs together
to produce a winding wondrous web.

The crisp of the frost layered my feet
as if my slippers were covered in cloud.

Twigs take off their cloaks of leaves.

The full moon thins the evening sun
as night begins.

Joshua Towell (11)
St James' RC Primary School, Orpington

One Monday Morning . . .

One Monday morning when the sky was grey,
I was ready for school and on my way.
When something in the corner caught my eye,
It was twinkling like stars in the night sky.
A teleporting hole made from glittery star dust,
I thought to myself, *shall I go? Oh I must.*
I climbed in the hole, wind rushed through my hair,
The feeling was so delightful, I didn't have a care.
Eventually I got to a magical land,
Where pixies and elves danced hand in hand.
One saw me, pointed and yelled,
'It's a human, that's what we smelled.'
They gathered around me and together they said,
'Come with us,' and away I was led.
Toadstools with tiny windows and doors,
And a tiny bed where one elf snores.
Three mischievous pixies in miniscule hats,
Were playing a game with raindrops and bats.
A rainbow reflected in their sea,
Made of lemonade and herbal tea.
The sky was cloudless and looked so fine,
Unlike the world I left behind.
With these creatures I made such great friends,
We laughed for hours, end on end.
But I knew I had to go home,
To the streets I used to roam.
I said goodbye but they will learn
That I will very soon return.

Bethany Meehan (10)
St James' RC Primary School, Orpington

The Shopping Trip

You may have heard of bad shopping trips,
But this one was just weird,
The first thing I saw in the market,
Was a live mouse with a beard!

There were sticky spiderwebs,
Spiders with them too,
And out of the corner of my eye,
I'm sure I saw an egg from the kangaroo!

Snail slime for only £9.99,
I'd throw them in the bin,
Wolf fur for only £15.99,
Now that's a bargain!

Our shopping trolley was full
With lots of revolting things,
We even had fox saliva,
Made into a drink.

Although Dad said rats' eggs make you thinner,
I didn't want to eat my dinner,
Also there were shaved chickens and hens,
I didn't want to go there again.

Ashley Whyte (10)
St James' RC Primary School, Orpington

Goal!

Football, football is in my soul
Nothing makes me happier than when I score a goal
In all sorts of weather
We play on together
Ignoring the frostbite, the cold, the rain
Not forgetting the injuries, the cuts and the pain
The best feeling is when I score
And I want to play it more and more.

Dominic Murrell (10)
St James' RC Primary School, Orpington

Autumn

The birds sing their song to the listening flowers.
My voice is the breath of the wind.
My cloak is the leaves crunching together.
The trees wave in my power.
My hands pick up the brown leaves.

Tom Roberts (10)
St James' RC Primary School, Orpington

African Prince

The mighty one,
Stood tall and proud,
Amongst other predators prowled.

Muscles bulged for all to see,
Curled talons clawed dirt,
Amber slits intimidate subjects.

Deafening roars shake the rotting trees,
Africa bows before him,
As do creatures of land and sea.

Incisors snatch up petrified prey,
Prince of Africa engulfed in glory,
For he is the lion!

Angela Wilby (11)
St James' RC Primary School, Orpington

An Autumn Day

The gingered leaves cry out as they leave their mother.
She stands tall and proud.
Staring berries watch the crisp leaves disguise the swaying grass.
Icy winds spread winter's despair.
They travel the world only to find angry clouds and armoured trees.
Thin, prickled branches clatter and echo against each other,
Waving and calling in the wind.
Birds scour the Earth in search of a warm, shining sea,
Going from dismal, dreary country to dismal, dreary country.
The clear sky watches over and listens, waiting to pounce.
All is silent!

Jamie Williams (11)
St James' RC Primary School, Orpington

Autumn

Who am I?
The crunching leaves are my cloak,
The wandering dew is the teardrops falling from my eyes.

Who am I?
The song of the birds is my hushed voice,
The mud is muffling the squelching of my shoes.

Who am I?
The wind pushes the golden leaves off the detached trees,
Swaying trees are my hands reaching out towards me.

Who am I?
The roots of trees are dancing ballerinas
And the soil is twisting and turning.

Who am I?
Still do not know?
I am Autumn.

Jodie Williams (10)
St James' RC Primary School, Orpington

Autumn Senses

My voice is the gusty wind,
Blowing the leaves off the trees,
Piling them high on the pavements,
Swirling them around in the sky.

My tears are the droplets of rain,
Falling on hill and on plain,
Saying goodbye to the summer,
Until it returns again.

My cloak is the cloudy sky,
Time for the birds to fly,
Away to the south,
Goodbye, goodbye.

Danielle Woolston (10)
St James' RC Primary School, Orpington

Vibrant Southern Lights

Ghostly vivid lights dance their way along the lightened sky,
Stars glimmer through the transparent eerie lights,
The atmospheric buildings being lit up by illuminescent green lights
While stars rest peacefully in a blanket of darkness.

Atmosphere fills the dull night sky,
Stars shoot across the sky, filling it with light,
Bright lights on the bold building reflect into the sky,
Radiant green gloomy lights fill the sky with joy.
Stars lay quietly in the sky,
Causing an astronomical display.

Amber Fenton-Scott (10)
Snodland CE Primary School, Snodland

Aurora Borealis

A tmospheric lights fighting for attention.
U nderstanding stars gazing down on the frozen paradise below.
R esistant lights keeping guard of the night sky.
O ver the ice the seeking stars sleep.
R ival winds rapidly battle in the moonlight stars.
A urora Borealis, dancing to the voice of the wind.

B right colours ablaze in the sky.
O verhead buildings towering the little town below.
R ising stars shooting across the midnight skies.
E normous dumbstruck building stopped in the mild air.
A mazing moonlight hit the town like a bus' headlights
L asting, forever the moonlight shone like an angel.
I ntimidating night sky spread out wide.
S hining stars took the last breath as night fell.

Lorenzo Heath (11)
Snodland CE Primary School, Snodland

Aurora

A mazing aurora
U ninhabited forgotten land
R apid lights float across the sky
O rnate light dances through the rough night sky
R oaring winds scatter snow towards the aurora
A ttention seeking stars trapped behind the magic green light.

Brady Moss (10)
Snodland CE Primary School, Snodland

The Aurora Australis

Vibrant green lights dance magically,
Illuminating the dark night sky.
Eyes twinkle with amazement
At this magical performance.

The ghostly green lights do a balletic performance
Over the isolated landscape.

The building stands alone
Watching the aurora's performance.

Shannon Lovett (11)
Snodland CE Primary School, Snodland

In The Fields

Poppies grow in the fields,
Whose past makes people wince,
There was a war here years ago,
It's seen no human since.

The people here were fighting,
With guns and bombs and tanks,
When soldiers came home healthy,
Their families gave thanks.

Charlotte Smith (11)
Snodland CE Primary School, Snodland

Ghostly Green

Amazing lights jump around in the bright night sky
And move like a heavenly performance.

The newborn stars in the sky
Trying to break through the lights and be seen.

The dark black sky illuminated
By the ghostly green lights.

Reece Roser (10)
Snodland CE Primary School, Snodland

A Green Wonder

A green scary snake slithers across the night sky,
Huge buildings gaze in amazement
As the lights give a balletic-like performance,
The shining stars are as white as snow,
Glimmering in the night sky.

Jamie Barden (10)
Snodland CE Primary School, Snodland

Australis

Beautiful bold gases light up the night sky,
The unbelievable green luminous gases cover the night,
A ghost covers the town and haunts the people below,
Like an alien spaceship has gone over the South Pole,
The astonishing stars in the sky,
Eventually the stars got to show off in the night,
Big bold building under the astonishing night sky,
The lights of the building are nowhere near as bright as the stars.

Robbie Manser (10)
Snodland CE Primary School, Snodland

The Sound Collector

(Based on 'The Sound Collector' by Roger McGough)

As I heard the door creak,
Everything froze, including the tap leak.
He illuminated my house with the sight of daylight,
My house is now extremely bright!

Into his sack went my cereal crunch,
In other words my morning munch,
The bathroom door slams,
The cooking pots clam,
The sound of my morning moans,
Then the drain groans,
The sound of the letter box's bang,
As the morning birds sang,
Into his sack he stuffed the sounds,
Sounds of my life from all around!

Lucy-Jane Letford (10)
Snodland CE Primary School, Snodland

Ghostly Green Light

Ghostly green lights magically dance through the night sky,
Glimmering stars vie for attention
Like a small flower tries its best to be seen,
The dark black stage stands very still
As the amazing green light performs
In front of all the stars in the sky.

Xena Mounteney (11)
Snodland CE Primary School, Snodland

Atmosphere Aurora

A mazing Aurora gazing down at the dark building,
T winkling stars are eerie,
M agical Aurora,
O utstanding Aurora,
S lithering Aurora,
P eaceful Aurora,
H eavenly Aurora,
E xtraordinary stars,
R ushing stars,
E xultant Aurora,

A stonishing Aurora,
U nbelievable glow,
R adiant Aurora,
O vert stars,
R ushing stars,
A stronomical Aurora.

Kiera Anderson (11)
Snodland CE Primary School, Snodland

Arctic Poem

Menacing shadows surround the incredible ice cave,
Sharp shimmering icicles glow in the superb sunlight,
Colossal golden sun shines like a beacon showing the way,
Inuit hunters give a baleful glance at a wonderful white polar bear,
Immensely deep ice covers the extremely frozen ground,
Slowly travellers saunter through the thick blanket of snow,
Soft, silky, snow covers the whole ground like a soft mattress.

Daniel Thomas (10)
Snodland CE Primary School, Snodland

Arctic Poem

I saw the bright sunshine in the glimmery blue ice cave.
I saw distant travellers waddling on the crunchy hard snow.
As the ice melts the light gets stronger and stronger and stronger.
As the colossal cave looks out in the open
It looks like it has got teeth and a one-eyed monster monstrosity.
Slowly the old people started to slow down
As the unstoppingly cold drops lower and lower.
It looked like an avalanche happened
And at the top of the cave was a gigantic, giant mountain.
As all the land awoke the horizon came up.

Callum Penn (9)
Snodland CE Primary School, Snodland

Arctic Poem

Mysterious icicles surround like evil guards.
Shining under the hot sun, lies soft silky snow on the freezing ground.
Beautiful colours shimmer just like a rainbow in the sky.
The burning sun sparkles in the light blue sky.
Cold travellers have loads of snow in their freezing cold boots.
Blue sky shines like a thousand stars in the sky.
So soft snow surrounds the land with the dark blue sea,
With a layer of milk on top of the sea, just like ice.
Healthy travellers plod across the crunchy snow.
Beautiful ice sparkles in the sunlight.

Natasha Smith (10)
Snodland CE Primary School, Snodland

Snowy Landscape

Sharply, the long crystal-like icicles shine
Like a star in the shimmering sun.
Scarily, the icicles are murderous as their silhouette falls.
Meanwhile, as the magical horizon falls level
With the smooth, snowy landscape,
I feel a spark of happiness cover the unforgettable scene.
Through a tiny hole in the eerie dark ice cave,
I capture a glimpse of the colossal, sparkling sun moving calmly.

Nathan Thomas (10)
Snodland CE Primary School, Snodland

Arctic Poem

Shadowy figures appear from the shiny shimmering sun.
Icicles drip like rain falling from the sky,
They are knives hanging from string.
Untouched landscape stays still like a statue.
Slowly walking on the snow is like walking in the air.
The snow is crunchy, soft, freezing and silky.
As I look at the sky I feel that the sky is saying hi.

Harry Gearing (10)
Snodland CE Primary School, Snodland

Poem About The Arctic

The soft, silver, silky snow
As all the peeking people get down low.
Slowly all the icicles drop
But all the smooth silky snow always likes to sop.
As the colossal cave wears out
All the travellers move about.
The shimmering sun shines so bright,
It is also shining with all its might.
All of the people find some food
Some of which are in a bad mood.
A few of the travellers are making friends
Some of them wearing new trends.
As all the ice begins to melt
All the ice will not be felt.

Alex Pollington (9)
Snodland CE Primary School, Snodland

Untitled

Imperial shadows surround the icy entrance
Like the Prime Minister's bodyguard,
Icicles like spears hang greatly over the icy entrance,
People take their time, watching the amazing view,
Slowly the shimmering sun tries and tries to melt the snow.

Billy Miners (10)
Snodland CE Primary School, Snodland

Mysterious Ice Cave

Menacing shadows surround the glimmering ice cave.
Thick snow is as white as a fluffy cloud.
The dazzling sun beams through the shiny ice.
Icicles fall to the ground like lightning hitting a tree.
Incredible icy icicles are as sharp as a knitting needle.

Sky is as blue as the deep colossal sea.
Blue like ice is a cave with icicles as long as a giraffe's neck.
Icicles at the front of the cave hang there like bats.

Inuits pass by as the sky, that is like a glimmering sapphire, passes them.

Katie Hooker (10)
Snodland CE Primary School, Snodland

Arctic Secrets

Slowly the sun flickered
Suddenly the bitter cold ice freezes
Strongly the mysterious shadow lurked around the ice cave
Scrunchy, silky snow turned to ice like lightning
Wind whipped widely around like a cheetah
Prancing snow leapt across the colossal snow cave
Intrepid travellers fought the furious wind
Decrepit snow melted slowly into freezing water
Baleful wind crashed against the ice.

Grace Carter (9)
Snodland CE Primary School, Snodland

Icy Cave

Icicles, shimmering in the golden sun,
While the bitter winds whip around the sparkling ice,
Meanwhile the crystal blue sky towers over the frozen sea,
The sun beaming into the magical ice cave like a laser.

On the frozen sea it looks like a glacier.
Icicles that look like vampires' teeth drop water
Like blood running down a knife.
Glimmering, soft, silky snow looks like a sheet of ice.
Will anyone ever discover this wonderful place?

Joe Murrell (9)
Snodland CE Primary School, Snodland

Untitled

The shimmering sun shines down onto the icicles
As the people walk along the fluffy white snow.
Snowflakes fall from the sky.
Animals lie still in the winter wonderland.
The snow is as white as the fluffy clouds.
Biting cold gets to you like tiny flies eating you.
Colossal ice blocks appear from nowhere.

Shannon Doig (9)
Snodland CE Primary School, Snodland

Snowy Arctic

Slowly the shimmering snow sparkled like a burning star
Creepily the colossal icicles creeped a traveller like a shark
Dangerously the immense glacier was bitter as the furious polar bear
Quickly the soft sparkly snow is shimmering in the sunlight
Noisily the creepy sea ice shone in the moonlight
Carefully the intrepid travellers trod through the soft silky snow.

Hannah Keightley (10)
Snodland CE Primary School, Snodland

Untitled

The sharp icicles point like needles.
Crunchy snow as white as rice.
Icy sea as cold as a freezer.
Glimmering sun melting a secret ice cave.
Blue shimmering sky shining down on the snow.

Hannah Bourke (9)
Snodland CE Primary School, Snodland

Arctic Cave

The shimmering icicles shining
in the sparkling sun like a crystal.
I see the shining in the sky,
as bright as a star.
A magical cave lies on its own,
ever so mysteriously.

Zachery Chambers (9)
Snodland CE Primary School, Snodland

Untitled

The shining sun shimmering like a bomb exploding in the blue sky.
Icicles glimmering like a knife reflecting off the fireball sun.
White everywhere, candyfloss shining in the sun.
Inuits walking in white polar bear skins, brown seal skins for their boots.
As the colossal cave melts water falls from the top.
Slowly the ice melts, the snow melts
Because the glimmering sun is shining on the Arctic.
White snow relaxing like a human relaxing in Egypt.

Alexander Freeman (10)
Snodland CE Primary School, Snodland

The Snake

I have a venomous tongue,
I am not normally fun.
The adder and I are family,
We do not like the sea
Because it is salty.
I am scaly, slithery and sneaky,
I am also very freaky.
If you see a boa constrictor
You will go, 'Eeky eeky!'
I will go *ssss* as well
To defend myself.
There is a grass snake in my garden.
I am a slithery snake, oops, pardon!

Matthew Kashman (8)
The Daiglen School, Buckhurst Hill

The Snake Of India

Slimy, sandy and scary.
Vicious, long and scaly.
Wide, curly, Indian snake, thin.
Intelligent, deadly or friendly.
Quick, fast and deadly.
Some can camouflage.
My venom is sticky
But I am quiet and careful.

Kalvin Matharu (8)
The Daiglen School, Buckhurst Hill

Will The Lion Make It?

Jumping through the long green grass, as long as anything could be
Fighting for his family's health
Thinking of nothing but his baby lion and lioness
Hoping the hunter won't find him, but will his wish come true?
Seeing his hut in the distance,
Smelling the hunter's gun, seeing a glimpse of one fast fiery bullet
Heading towards him and his feast.
Trying hard not to get hit and make it home to eat the feast
Crying for he's nearly dead, now Mother can see his sweating face
One last jump to the hut, made it to the safety of the hut.

Emma Jones (8)
The Daiglen School, Buckhurst Hill

The Emerald Jewel

As shiny as the glittery stars,
As green as the fresh grass,
Like a stunning crown in the light,
It shimmers like the golden sun far, far away,
Crystal clear like the sky on a sunny day,
As light as a feather,
As beautiful as a ruby,
It twinkles on a window sill,
You see the green light through the warm, cosy curtains,
It's a bright green torch,
It lights up the house when the clock strikes 12 o'clock,
I'm talking about an emerald jewel.

Brooke Vexler (8)
The Daiglen School, Buckhurst Hill

Darkness

Alone on a misty, dingy hike,
No food, no water, just a lengthening, tiresome walk,
The wind ferociously crashed on top of the foreboding mountains,
No life in this tranquil place with a treacherous path,
An apparition endeavouring to creep upon you,
Curiosity stalking your every step,
Darkness cloaks the craggy land,
Shifting shadows, moody mists, rumbling rains,
Oh where's my haven to rest my weary head?
Sleeping lonesomely without a tent,
You wake up quickly, a chilling touch on your skin,
Mysterious, gloomy ghosts lurking around
And you become intimidated,
And you run away from the terror
Hoping that you will never meet again.

Riyan Pillai (9)
The Daiglen School, Buckhurst Hill

Double Trouble

I walked slowly, head pointing to the ground,
When, suddenly I heard a spooky sound.
It was a cobra!
A rat, he did gobble,
But after a moment
His teeth started to wobble.
Suddenly I realised,
I was really in trouble.
I saw another snake that made my trouble, double!

Arjan Rattan (8)
The Daiglen School, Buckhurst Hill

Tenerife

Tenerife, so hot,
Glimmering in the sky,
Like shooting stars,
Big hotels like skyscrapers,
Different language like Spanish,
Lots of shops like crowds of people,
Bright blue sky like the ocean,
Hot beaches, hot as a barbecue,
Lots of crops such as bananas.

Elbert Barr (8)
The Daiglen School, Buckhurst Hill

The Flamey Fog

I stood there watching the freaky view
Until I felt like someone was tickling me
I looked behind and there I saw a flamey fog
It slid around me like it was part of me
It made my eyesight blur
It pushed me down to the icy floor
I could have yelled help but it was no use
There I lay without any life
I wished I was alive
But the wish was not answered.

Tsega Shawo (8)
The Daiglen School, Buckhurst Hill

The White Shark

I'm an underwater killer,
I share with none of the other fish,
I'm a shiny sight to the other fish,
My favourite food is crab and garden salad,
I will kill you with one bite,
Never come next to me because I will kill you!

Isaac Kirwan (7)
The Daiglen School, Buckhurst Hill

The Fierce Shark

I'm fierce, deadly and scary,
I'm silver and white and fast,
I am a fish eater and a human eater,
I'm freaky, giant and fearless,
I'm sharp, soft and smooth.

Max Rich (7)
The Daiglen School, Buckhurst Hill

The Snake Of War

Deadly, extremely long,
I'm vicious, sneaky and fast,
We live in hot, hot places,
And I'll strangle all day long,
So never take a holiday unless you're very careful
And I might come in for a tangle,
And I'm really furious about meat.

Amelie Baldwin (7)
The Daiglen School, Buckhurst Hill

Speed

As fast as a cheetah,
Like a lightning bolt,
Like blurred vision as you yawn,
Butterflies in your stomach,
As massive as a motorbike,
Fury like the Vikings,
Whistling past like a bullet!

Jacob Bukhari (9)
The Daiglen School, Buckhurst Hill

No One Knows . . .

No one knows . . .
That I can jump higher than a skyscraper,
That I can speak Chinese,
That I can shrink with a hat,
That I can run 9,000 miles without stopping.

No one knows . . .
That I own a palace,
That I have a plane,
That I have nine lives,
That I have every single game in the whole wide world.

Faizaan Mohammad Akhtar (8)
The Daiglen School, Buckhurst Hill

The Mountain Climb

Darkness falls upon the ground
The wind falls upon me
The wind whispers a deathly song
I feel as though I might as well give in
I hope and pray that I win.

Isobel Eastmond (8)
The Daiglen School, Buckhurst Hill

Excuses

I was sitting at home on my bright silver couch
When along came my dog and sat on my pouch.
He brought in my school bag
And opened it up
And all of a sudden he ripped it all up.
I went into school and explained to my teacher
She didn't believe me so she gave me a lecture.

Akram Sattar (9)
The Daiglen School, Buckhurst Hill

The Tiger Wolf

He has teeth like razors
They hurt you like tazers

He eats lots of meat
And he almost gets killed by the heat

He hides near a waterfall in the jungle
This beast is very humble

This beast is very smart
And that is why it has a good heart.

Dylan Pitter (9)
The Daiglen School, Buckhurst Hill

No Mum

Come and do your homework
No Mum

Come and wash the windows
No Mum

I'll give you a reward
No Mum

Come and tidy your room
No Mum

Come and wash the car
No Mum

Come and give me a hug
Yes Mum.

Lucas Jefcoate (10)
The Daiglen School, Buckhurst Hill

The Bloodsucking Snake

Bitter, bendy, black and deadly
Legless, armless, it's so not harmless.
Silvery, scary, scaly, sucker, skinny, smooth, strong and spotty.
Forest in India, fast, curly, red and black
I am poisonous too,
I am not harmless so beware!

Ayda May Alpaslan (7)
The Daiglen School, Buckhurst Hill

The Deadly Snake

I'm cheeky and freaky,
Everybody thinks I am leaky,
I am deadly, intelligent
And multicoloured.
I feel slimy and terrifying,
I am the darkest, most horrible
And I love chocolate cake,
I'm a brave killer
And I love my dinner.

Benjamin Charles Fletcher (7)
The Daiglen School, Buckhurst Hill

The Slimy Snake

Slithery, slimy but then a bit smooth,
I'm a snake that's on the loose,
I'm scary and slimy, I'm sort of flat,
I'm deadly and I'm long,
But I'm nowhere near as big as King Kong,
But sometimes I'm kind and sometimes I'm fun,
Sorry, gotta go,
The hunters, here they come!

Daniel Grogan (8)
The Daiglen School, Buckhurst Hill

The Bloodsucking Snake

It's from America,
It's the darkest creature in the forest,
It's always sucking blood from rats,
It's always eating my chocolate cake,
It looks at me sharply,
The Indian rats are the best to eat,
Nothing else,
I can camouflage and it's the best!
Slinking all day long across the grass.

Chloe Fletcher (7)
The Daiglen School, Buckhurst Hill

My Baby Sister

My baby sister who is one year old
Jia is gentle as a lamb who likes to explore
She makes me run around
And sometimes pushes me on the ground
She hums like a bird and swims like a fish
She crawls like a tortoise and jumps like a kangaroo
When she is in a bad mood she doesn't eat her food
I love my little sister, who is cuddly and cute.

Devak Rattan (10)
The Daiglen School, Buckhurst Hill

The Snake

I am a long, poisonous, sneaky snake,
So you better watch out for my deadly bite,
Shiny and fast I camouflage too,
My brain is intelligent so you better make yours too,
My scary patterned skin is beautifully thin,
So if you ever go to the rainforest
Keep an eye out for my slimy skin.

Safah Siddique (8)
The Daiglen School, Buckhurst Hill

The Race

Clark waited at the start line.
His engine as quiet as a mouse.
The flags went down.
Red then green like a traffic light.
Engines roared like lions.
They all sped off as fast as lightning.
Whirling round the bend like the wind.
Clark could see the finish line.
He was going as fast as a cheetah.
The flag came down.
Clark had won.
He started laughing like a hyena.

Clark Pollins (9)
The Daiglen School, Buckhurst Hill

The Bump

The Bump lived in the dump,
Scratching his itchy hump.
He twiddled his goosp,
And whacked his hooph,
And cried for his mum.

The Bump lived in the dump,
Stirring his gumpy-humf.
He whirled his goopynoop,
Clumpered his roopeydoop,
And hurled for his brum.

The Bump lived in the dump,
Scrambling his wicketyclump.
He fiddled his noosp,
And clacked his tooth,
And scrambled off in the sun.

Max Beaney (9)
The Daiglen School, Buckhurst Hill

A Fool At School

I woke up one morning
I felt like a fool
Oh no, no, no
I had to go to school.

I dressed into my clothes
My mum ate my chocolate bar
I didn't have any breakfast
So I ate my mum's car.

When I reached school
I said bye to my mum
Then I just remembered
I forgot my precious drum.

Everyone laughed at me
They called me a fool
I guess that in the morning
I was right after all.

Humza Hussain (9)
The Daiglen School, Buckhurst Hill

Cyprus

My first visit to Cyprus I shall never forget
The smell in the air so fresh
Friendly smiles everywhere
Something I found so rare
Whilst driving down the road
I saw sights beautiful
Making me appreciate God's creation
I saw mountains on my right
Standing like tall giants
Peering down at me
Making me smile
The sea gleaming in the sun
Shining on everyone
Making me feel warm
And wanting to return
To this wonderful place
Again and again.

Muizz Ali (9)
The Daiglen School, Buckhurst Hill

Graceful Egypt

This country is amazing, the people really are too
Their life is so different to the likes of me and you
They don't earn much money but still have a smile on their face
They walk around in shabby clothes but manage to hold such grace
I have spent a week in Egypt, a country full of history
The Sphinx, pyramids, Tutankhamun, everything a mystery
The leader of Egypt stayed in power for over thirty years
Yet when he stepped down you could hear the happy cheers
People praying around me, really causing no harm
I really hope Egypt can get on with life and remain calm
Children selling jewellery, so much younger than me
Nothing but sand, no clean water you can see
I love this country, Egypt, and it's really got me thinking
Visiting this incredible place has really touched my feelings.

Jordan Austen (11)
The Daiglen School, Buckhurst Hill

What Is The Cloud?

A cloud is a giant fluff ball moving slowly
It is like a puff of dust from the remains of a fallen city
A cloud is a white elephant storming the blue sky
It is like a moving desert in the dark sky
A cloud is a huge storm dominating the sky
But actually a cloud is water ready to fall.

Judson Rabey (10)
The Daiglen School, Buckhurst Hill

A Silly Zombie Poem

Silly zombie chasing me.
Silly zombie, can't you see?

I've got a gun fully loaded
And some bombs unexploded.

I've got to go and set your trap
So you can take a true dirt nap.

I love to shoot you so much
Or beat you to death with a crutch.

Silly zombie, say goodbye.
Silly zombie, you just died.

Harrison Wright (10)
The Daiglen School, Buckhurst Hill

The Forgiving Nan

I went to the front door
And smashed my nan right to the floor
I said she had a whisky shot
So she fell over onto the wooden cot
I left my nan right there and went to wash my greasy hair!

I went downstairs and saw the blood
So later on I mixed it with mud
My grandpa came up out of his grave
And shot my best mate, Dave.

I ate a giant chocolate bar
I realised it was tar!
Later on my nan told me
That she wasn't pleased with me!

I told her that it wasn't my fault
So I made her a wooden fort
For once she was pleased with me
Because she was my forgiving nan!

Lee Cavanagh (11)
The Daiglen School, Buckhurst Hill

Why?

I have always wondered why the sky is so high,
Or why trees are in the ground when they could be in a cloud?
Or why the grass is green and the sky is blue?
So I ask, why?
My oh my, only nature knows why . . .
Or is it that it is just how it's supposed to be?
That is why I ask why.

Shivam Kotecha (11)
The Daiglen School, Buckhurst Hill

Lifetime

I used to eat my father's shoes
'Cause my brother ate the blues

My cat just cut the titanium ridge
After my sister drank the bridge

Africa's time is Burma's line
My valentine was in the skyline

My sister said the Holy Grail
Was simply just blackmail

My email was a nature trail
Made for a monorail

The fairy queen was my windscreen
Who came between the unforeseen

Mum was a chrysanthemum
Acting like the millennium

The vitamin was a tiger skin
Bearskin, break-in, rolling pin

The brine was really quite divine
Which was terribly my guideline

My tea time was a crime
At a pantomime . . . sometimes

Harvest time, party time
Half-time, full-time, lifetime!

Dominic Williamson-Strachan (11)
The Daiglen School, Buckhurst Hill

War On Water

Two armies on the river
Both eating their own liver.
Walking and driving and flying too
Screaming and shouting the word moo.

Firing the pins off the grenades
And making bullets out of shade.
Letting the fish drink in gallons
While putting themselves in the cannons.

Driving planes, dropping fish
While thinking that they are swish.
There is no hope of anyone winning
Because everyone is dead from singing.

They're still fighting under the river
Hearing the sound of the zither.
Their hearts and souls will rest at peace
While living under floating geese.

Thomas Murray (11)
The Daiglen School, Buckhurst Hill

Sometimes

Sometimes at school I feel lonely
Sometimes I'm surrounded by friends
Sometimes I wish that school was finished
Sometimes I wish it would never end
Sometimes I think school is boring
Sometimes I think it's really fun
Sometimes I'm feeling fine
Sometimes I want to escape and run.

Molly Goddard (10)
Wethersfield CE (VC) Primary School, Wethersfield

Dad

My dad was very good at Xbox 360 games
My brothers and I have brown hair just like him.

He took me for fish and chips
We got a battered sausage and small chips
We ate them together in the car
It made the car smell for a long time.

He had a BMW
It was the colour blue
It used to stop when he was driving it
It always made him angry and annoyed.

Sometimes I dream of him
All of the stuff we did together
He is always in my thoughts
He was here, now he is gone.

Kelvin Girdlestone (9)
Wethersfield CE (VC) Primary School, Wethersfield

One Dark Night

Running down the road at night
Not knowing what's in sight,
I trip, blood is pouring from my knee,
Now I'm scared, I feel a hand!

It pulls on my shoe,
It slips, I start to run,
I look behind me and all I can see
Is a pair of red eyes staring back at me!

Shay Durell (11)
Wethersfield CE (VC) Primary School, Wethersfield

The World As We Know It

The sun was beating down on me
The waves washing upon the shore
As I lay, I lay today,
I lay for evermore.

The brushing sand on my shoulder blades
The seagulls look like they're playing charades
As I got up with a crunch in my tread,
I felt so down and lowered my head.

As I walk through the footprints of the past
The world moves around me ever so fast
Think of the world, the world like no other,
Destroyed and buried, a world not to bother.

George Squires (10)
Wethersfield CE (VC) Primary School, Wethersfield

Holiday Fun

H olidays are the best
O ver the world people go on holiday
L ovely sunny days
I just love eating every day
D rinking cocktails
A nd sunbathing by the pool
Y ou and your friends watching a show

F un for everyone
U nder the palm tree
N ice and quiet.

Amy Thomas (9)
Wethersfield CE (VC) Primary School, Wethersfield

The Sudden Cry

We are all at school
And I'm looking like a fool,
We all sit down
And look at our teacher in his gown,
When we hear a sudden cry,
Like a deer that's about to die,
We can tell it is in pain
So we run out with a cane,
'Look, it's over there!'
'Sleep well my friend, take care.'

Imogen Cayley (10)
Wethersfield CE (VC) Primary School, Wethersfield

When I Fell

I fell down a hole
And squashed a mole
I saw its soul
Rise high above
I knew it was dead
Then I said,
'Oh no,'
As some coal
Fell down the hole
And buried me dead!

Alex Robertshaw (11)
Wethersfield CE (VC) Primary School, Wethersfield

Strike

I was running, I could not see it
And it was fast and very deadly
Lots of people die from it

3000 volts of electricity.

Harry Stock (10)
Wethersfield CE (VC) Primary School, Wethersfield

Favourite Things

F avourite things are things like:
A nimals and wildlife,
V olleyball and sport,
O utside in the garden,
U nder an umbrella,
R iding on your bike,
I rritating your big sister,
T aking all the sweets,
E ating all the food,

T aking your brother's new football,
H itting around a ball,
I nside watching telly,
N apping on the beach,
G etting sweets from the shop,
S inging and dancing around the house.

Louise Wilkins (9)
Wethersfield CE (VC) Primary School, Wethersfield

Australia

A nimals in the trees all around,
U nder the soil, a spider burrows,
S nakes hide in the shadows, waiting for prey,
T he sun, shining brightly in the sky,
R eefs surrounding the country,
A borigines, celebrating around camp fires,
L ittle creatures hide in the undergrowth,
I ndian Ocean and other seas filled with coral,
A ustralia is brilliant.

Joe Nichols (10)
Wethersfield CE (VC) Primary School, Wethersfield

Down The Hole

I fell down a hole,
Which was filled with coal
And with a fright
I punched with might
At a rat
Which turned out to be
A very fat cat.
I turned around and then I found
Loads of skulls
And a bunch of dead seagulls,
Then I hit my head
Then thought to myself
In a cosy bed,
Then I said,
'I must be dead!'

Liam Cooper (10)
Wethersfield CE (VC) Primary School, Wethersfield

Bertie The Bassett Hound

Bertie the dirty Bassett Hound
Trips over his own ears when he runs around,
He runs with great excitement
To see me when I get home from school.
He jumps for a cuddle,
I think he's really cool.

Sullivan Tyler-Holman (11)
Wethersfield CE (VC) Primary School, Wethersfield

Matthew

He had blonde hair
And he was really tall and funny.
Always trying to make you laugh.

He was 11 years old,
A funny situation was when he ran into a tree.
His name was Matthew.

He had his arm broken
And it was all up to me,
So I picked him up and ran him home.

He came to school the next day
With his arm in a cast.

Bailey Tyler (11)
Wethersfield CE (VC) Primary School, Wethersfield

Old Red Riding Hood

The sun was shining on the wood,
An old woman was wearing her hood,
In her red Ferrari she stood,
She was lost in the big wide wood,
She was Little Red Riding Hood's nan,
'Wow! I am such a fan!'
She was heading her way to Little Red's house,
Just then along scurried a mouse,
Two wolves were blocking her way,
All of a sudden they shouted, 'Stay!'
She accelerated right through the block,
Then she realised there was a lock,
Little Red opened the door and gave her cookies,
She asked for more,
This is my poem, I hope it wasn't a bore.

Perhan Olmazu (11)
Woodford Green Primary School, Woodford Green

Rapunzel

Her hair as long as the tower,
She'd been waiting for many an hour,
Her eyes were as sweet as honey,
But the wait was not so funny,
Along came the prince in his handsome silk coat,
But he couldn't get to her because of the crocodile moat,
He tried to get to her but could not float,
But with a stroke of luck there was an old wooden boat,
He rescued his princess by climbing her hair,
She said, 'Good to see you but please use the stairs!'

Jemima Rodriguez Salt (10)
Woodford Green Primary School, Woodford Green

The Gingerbread Man

There once was a kind old baker,
Who was a great bread maker,
She made a gingerbread man,
Who ran and ran and ran,
He jumped right out of the door.
And straight onto the floor,
A cat was passing by,
And saw the ginger man fly,
Fly right down the road,
So the cat followed,
A dog saw the chase,
And thought it was a race,
The gingerbread man came to a river,
And then he froze and started to quiver,
'What shall I do?
There is no way through.'
A fox heard the ginger man's cry,
And had a thought that was very sly,
'I will trick the gingerbread man,'
So the fox ran,
Ran right out from behind a bush,
And gave the ginger man a mighty push,
He pushed him onto the floor,
So the ginger man swore,
'I am not a type of meat,
That you usually eat!'
But the fox didn't listen
And its teeth started to glisten,
That was the last of the cheeky bread,
So keep this poem in your head!

Megan Bradley (11)
Woodford Green Primary School, Woodford Green

The Gingerbread Man

There was a baker called Old Fred,
Who decided to make a gingerbread.
He cooked him up in a red-hot pan,
'I'll call you the Gingerbread Man.'
He threw him on a big white plate,
'Shame on you, I'm gonna eat you mate!'
The gingerbread man jumped off the table,
'You can't catch me, I'm running to Mabel.
Run, run as fast as you can,
You can't catch me, I'm the Gingerbread Man.'
On his way he sat on a log,
And caught a glimpse of a slimy old frog.
The frog was bright and yellowy green,
And did not like the colour scheme.
The frog began to chase the pastry,
So the Gingerbread Man got a bit hasty.
The gingerbread passed a dancing tree
And came across a buzzing bee.
The bee began to fly so high
And so did the little guy.
'Let me down you stupid bee,
This won't be the last of me.'
The Gingerbread Man struggled around
And finally found a way to the ground.
Along came a fox,
Who was wearing high socks.
Even though the little man ran,
That was the last of the Gingerbread Man.

Ece Elmaz (11)
Woodford Green Primary School, Woodford Green

Bronzilocks And The Three Gold Bears

Once upon a time there were three gold bears,
They made porridge with some tasty pears.
Their porridge was too hot,
They left the porridge in a pot.
They left for a short, wanderous walk,
They walked to a forest called Green Chalk.

Bronzilocks came in a flash
And wanted to see if there was any cash.
She found some porridge in a bowl,
When she tasted it she started to call,
'This is too hot, this is too cold,
This is just right within my hold.'

Bronzilocks wanted a nice, old rest,
But she was scared to sleep here as she was a guest.
The bed wrinkled when Bronzilocks climbed,
She sang a little, short rap that rhymed,
'This is too soft, this is too hard,
This is just right for a bard.'
She slept there forgetting the time,
She didn't hear the clock starting to chime.

The gold bears came to eat their food,
They came with a good mood.
Baby Gold Bear saw the porridge and started to cry,
'Who ate my food, please don't lie.'

They went to the bedroom, their face red,
Bronzilocks was sleeping in little Gold Bear's bed.
She woke up with all the din,
And ran through the window into a bin.
That was the end of the cheeky bear,
She never came back with her nasty stare.

Varshini Thavakumar (10)
Woodford Green Primary School, Woodford Green

Sleeping Beauty

Sleeping Beauty fell down in bed
Oh no, is she dead?
The three fairies went away
They went to prison, it took all day
The fairies set free the prince, all of them fled
The army came, they went all red
'I'll fight them all,' the prince said
He took out his sword which was made of lead
The prince and fairies went up to the bridge
But they had a tiny hitch
It's closing, it's closing, it's closing, right up
'I have a plan.' He took out his arrow, 'Now duck!'
The blue arrow hit the gate
The army took his bait
They opened the gate without a second thought
The team ran straight through, coming into an old fort
Suddenly a huge talking dragon came down
'I'm going to kill you, I'll be bound.'
The prince stabbed the dragon right through the heart
'I killed you, I killed you,' as he jumped into the cart
He ran up through the tall tower
As he raced up the stairs holding a pretty red flower
The prince looked at the bed, there lay
The princess shining in the sun's ray
The princess was as ugly as can be
The prince heard a voice in his head, *please help me*
He went down in a kiss
She woke up in total bliss
They broke up in great big laughter
Beauty and the prince lived happily ever after.

Anduena Bardhi (10)
Woodford Green Primary School, Woodford Green

Little Legged Riding Hood

Once upon a time,
There was a girl worth a dime,
She wore a cloak of red,
With a hood upon her head,
And one day she went,
To her nan's house in Kent,
And finally when she got there,
Her nutty nan was covered in hair,
'Oh Nan!' Little Legged Riding Hood said,
And she threw the basket of food and fled,
Her nan jumped up
And grabbed a cup,
Little Legged Riding Hood ran as fast as she could,
But then she got lost in the big wood,
'I'm not your nan!'
And the wolf smacked her with a can,
Little Legged Riding Hood,
Fell to the ground of hard wood,
'Hmm, what a lovely treat!'
Said the wolf eating all the meat.

Amber Bracey (11)
Woodford Green Primary School, Woodford Green

The Gingerbread Man Mark II

There was a baker baking a gingerbread man,
When it was done the Gingerbread Man ran.
He got out of the oven blazing hot,
He hid in a large pot,
'Run, run as fast as you can,
You can't catch me because I'm the Gingerbread Man.'
He got him by a hook.
He gave him a big bad look.
When they got back to the bakery,
He hit him with a pan,
Then he put him in a big red van.

Baxter Joy (10)
Woodford Green Primary School, Woodford Green

Little Red Riding Hood

Tiny, little, brave Red Riding Hood
Went for a walk in the big wood
She took baskets of wine
For Nan who was not fine
Then she saw a wolf, this is not good!

Maariya Gonzalez Patel (10)
Woodford Green Primary School, Woodford Green

Aladdin With A Wish

A genie appeared and said,
'What do you wish for Sir?'
I errd and I ummed and I errd.
'I know, my first is to have a princess
And I want to buy her a golden dress.
My second wish is to have a flying carpet
One that is cool but not from the market!
My very last wish is to be king!
Plus a big fat diamond ring.'
'OK sir, I'll grant your wish
And for a present I give you a dish!'

Trinity Collins (11)
Woodford Green Primary School, Woodford Green

Untitled

Once upon a time,
In a world of fun and rhyme,
There were three little kitties,
And a dog who was a pity,
The kitties' mother died,
And the kitties, oh they cried,
So they needed to find a house,
But be as quiet as a mouse,
So they made a house of straw,
But there wasn't any door,
The dumb dog crept in,
And the kitties ran for their chinny chin chins,
And as the dog chased them,
He tripped on a flower stem,
Next they made a house of bricks,
But the kitties became sick,
So the dog broke through the door,
And there stood something more,
Bigger than the dog, 'cause there stood a lion,
After that the dog started cryin',
In the end it was fine,
The sun started to shine,
The dog stopped his crime,
In a world of fun and rhyme.

Saleh Salim (10)
Woodford Green Primary School, Woodford Green

The Story Of The Gingerbread Man

In memory of the Gingerbread Man,
Who was extremely easy to cook,
Dashed away in fear,
But now he is lost in a baker's big book.

Anton Barrett (10)
Woodford Green Primary School, Woodford Green

The Gingerbread Man

Once upon a time a cook baked bread.
A gingerbread man jumped out and hurt his head.
He ran and ran as fast as he can.
Then said, 'You can't catch me, I'm the Gingerbread Man.'
In shock and terror the cook got a book.
He was about to throw but then he shook.
The Gingerbread Man ran and ran.
He got hit by a speeding red van.
Quickly he got up, a woman put him in a cup.
She took him to lunch
Where the baker said, 'Munch, munch, munch!'

Junior Gichie (11)
Woodford Green Primary School, Woodford Green

Little Red Riding Hood

Little Red Riding Hood
Walked in the scary old wood
She saw the trees wave
As she entered a cave
She saw a wolf that was big and grey
Little Red Riding Hood just ran away
She ran and ran
When she saw her nan
With a frilly old hat on her head
When she thought she was dead
She turned around
The wolf was on the ground
She thanked the man
And gave him a fan.

Nazey Ozcan (10)
Woodford Green Primary School, Woodford Green

Gingerbread Man

There once was a gingerbread man
Who said, 'Run, run as fast as you can.'
The baker chased him
And kicked him in the bin
'I will take you home for my nan.'

Finnian Cunningham (11)
Woodford Green Primary School, Woodford Green

The Gingerbread Man

There was a gingerbread man,
Who ran as fast as he can,
He ran out through an open door,
He was definitely breaking the law,
Then he got eaten by a fox,
Which jumped out of the box,
And that was the end of Mr Ginger,
He really was quite a whinger!

Joshua Samuel Ball (11)
Woodford Green Primary School, Woodford Green

A Witch Sandwich

A witch sandwich is easy to make
All you do is simply take . . .
Ten dead bugs
And a cobwebby mug,
Thirteen dead squashed flies
And two disgusting eyes,
Three green germs
And two wiggly worms,
Thirteen ugly fleas
And two buzzing and stinging bees.
That ought to do it,
Now here comes the problem . . .
Biting into it!

Amber Terry (7)
Woodville Primary School, South Woodham Ferrers

Nightmares

Thoughts whirling round my head
I think they're coming true
I'm lying in my bed
And it's all a big hullabaloo
I think it's coming closer
I don't actually know
Whatever's there
Gives me the shivers from head to toe
Is it a bear?
A cat or a mouse?
All these funny sounds
And this funny house
It's like the howling of the hounds
But there's really nothing there
It's all just a dream
Or more like a nightmare.

Katherine Miles (10)
Woodville Primary School, South Woodham Ferrers

A Stocking

Fluffy and nice
And warm
Top made out of wool
Decoration
Sometimes stripy
And green and white
All lovely
With tinsel on
To stick on my fireplace.

Grace Wakefield (8)
Woodville Primary School, South Woodham Ferrers

My Favourite Story

My favourite story
Is luckily not gory,
It's called Goldilocks and the Three Bears,
But they prefer porridge than pears,
She steals porridge from the bears which is bad,
Yes it's true, she is mad,
Then Little Bear found out she'd broken his chair,
So he said, 'It's not fair!'
She walked upstairs to go to bed,
But the bears woke her up and then she fled,
She ran out to the wood,
Where she found Little Miss Riding Hood,
She was very sweet,
In a basket she had a very big treat,
The treat was for her gran
But they saw a wolf in the wood and ran,
Both of these stories are very good,
But I prefer the Three Bears than Little Miss Riding Hood.

Zoe Pilkington (10)
Woodville Primary School, South Woodham Ferrers

Stocking

Fluffy,
White, warm and soft
Frilly bits on the top
Shaped as a sack
They call it a stocking
Because it is a sock.

Taylah Cush (7)
Woodville Primary School, South Woodham Ferrers

Tree

Star
Tall, nice, sparkly.
Green
Decorated Christmas tree
With
Blue, red, orange lights
With
Little snowmen.
Present.

Benjamin Billings (7)
Woodville Primary School, South Woodham Ferrers

The Witch With A Twitch

One day,
I was walking through the woods in my own little way,
When I bumped into a witch,
Who had a terrible twitch.
She gave me such a fright,
Enough to send me running into the night.
Scrambling through the trees,
I started getting chased by some honeybees.

Running right to left,
I started to think I had met my death.
I shouted, 'Help!'
But no one was around to hear me yelp.
Just when I thought it was all going to end,
I saw my house around the bend.
I ran straight into my home,
I would never go out again alone!

Alice Rockliff (10)
Woodville Primary School, South Woodham Ferrers

Frankenstein

Never dine with Frankenstein
It will send a shiver down your spine
If it's food that you pine
Grab some grapes from a vine.

His manners are quite a sight
In fact they will give you a fright
All I can suggest is hold on tight
And turn off the light!

Frankie Smith (10)
Woodville Primary School, South Woodham Ferrers

A Dinosaur Sandwich

A dinosaur sandwich is easy to make.
All you do is simply take . . .
One big toad
And mud from the bucket load.
One human lung
And a spoonful of cow dung.
Two dead pigs
And a cow that digs.
That ought to do it.
Now here comes the problem . . .
Biting into it!

Jack Fisk (7)
Woodville Primary School, South Woodham Ferrers

A Witch Sandwich

A witch is easy to make.
All you do is simply take . . .
Two bat wings
And a cow that sings,
Two fish eyes
And ten dead flies,
One rotten sock
And a cobwebby clock.
That ought to do it,
Now comes the problem,
Biting into it!

Kyle Burgess (8)
Woodville Primary School, South Woodham Ferrers

Wizard

A wizard sandwich is easy to make,
All you do is simply take . . .
A wizard's wart,
A shark we caught,
An eagle's wing,
Seven cows that sing,
Ten dragon eyes,
Six slug pies,
That ought to do it,
And now comes the problem . . .
Biting into it!

Megan Johnson (8)
Woodville Primary School, South Woodham Ferrers

A Dinosaur Sandwich

A dinosaur sandwich is easy to make,
All you do is simply take . . .
Seven people's brains,
Two dinosaur veins,
Thirty-one flies,
Eighty-seven eyes,
Eight dead fleas,
Twenty hopping bees.
That ought to do it,
Now here comes the problem,
Biting into it!

Luke Piper (7)
Woodville Primary School, South Woodham Ferrers

A Witch Sandwich

A witch sandwich is easy to make,
All you do is simply take . . .
One fat slimy frog,
That was sitting on a log.
Three wriggly worms
That are covered in germs.
The wing of a bat,
The eye of a cat.
A lizard from a wizard
That was caught in a blizzard.
A bottle of blood,
That's as thick as mud.
A crocodile's rotten tooth
And a smelly old cow's hoof.
That ought to do it,
Now comes the problem . . .
Biting into it!

Sam Mason (7)
Woodville Primary School, South Woodham Ferrers

A Witch Sandwich

A witch sandwich is easy to make
All you do is simply take . . .
A spoonful of mud
A piece of spider blood
One dish of hay
And a piece of day
Add some nuts
And glass cups
Two cows' eyes
And a man's thighs
That ought to do it
Now here comes the problem . . .
Biting into it!

Grace Allen (8)
Woodville Primary School, South Woodham Ferrers

A Witch's Sandwich

A witch's sandwich is easy to make
All you do is simply take . . .
One cup of frog's blood for butter
With a dead butterfly that did flutter
Two big bat wings
A lizard that sings
Two eyes from a snake
A rusty rake
A dead snail
Guts from a whale
One melted caveman
Some oil from a van
A dead man's leg
And a sticky cobweb
That ought to do it
Now comes the problem . . .
Biting into it.

George Crouch (7)
Woodville Primary School, South Woodham Ferrers

Witch

A witch's sandwich is easy to make
All you do is simply take . . .
A beak from a bird
A lizard that I heard
Ten stingers from a bee
Six leaves from a tree
A manky glove
A mouldy apple from above
That ought to do it
Now comes the problem . . .
Biting into it!

Freya Ellis (7)
Woodville Primary School, South Woodham Ferrers

A Witch Sandwich

A witch sandwich is easy to make
All you do is simply take . . .
A slimy worm
That will make you squirm
A furry cat
That will make you a rat
A nice furry spider
That will make it hotter
A nice juicy child
That will make you wild
A piece of candy
It will come in handy
A crawling bug
And a slithering slug
That ought to do it
Now comes the problem . . .
Biting into it!

Nathan Laverack (7)
Woodville Primary School, South Woodham Ferrers

A Witch Sandwich

A witch sandwich is easy to make
All you do is simply take . . .
A cat that sings
Six dead birds' wings
One very, very smelly sock
Two very gooey clocks
A boy that is young
A girl that sung
That ought to do it
Now comes the problem . . .
Biting into it!

Jack Ashby (7)
Woodville Primary School, South Woodham Ferrers

A Dinosaur Sandwich

A dinosaur sandwich is easy to make
All you do is simply take . . .
Two slices of bread
One small human head
Four pig eyes
Ten flaming hot pies
Five small mice tails
One cat that smells
Seventeen very fast cars
One really big Mars
Fifteen very bright stars
Seven milk chocolate bars
Eleven hot dishes
Thirteen flapping fishes
That ought to do it
Now comes the problem . . .
Biting into it!

William Creak (7)
Woodville Primary School, South Woodham Ferrers

Witch

A witch sandwich is easy to make
All you do is simply take . . .
A slice of bread
And a frog's head
One slug
And a tiny bug
My pig's eye
And a fish about to die
One hissing snake
And a toad from the lake
Five bones
And a dog that moans
That ought to do it
Now here comes the problem . . .
Biting into it!

Alana Davies (8)
Woodville Primary School, South Woodham Ferrers

A Witch Sandwich

A witch sandwich is easy to make,
All you do is simply take . . .
One smelly potion,
Some suntan lotion.
Two spoonfuls of dung,
A rabbit's lung.
Three humans' legs,
Six wooden pegs.
One snake's tail,
A metal pail.
Seven mouldy socks,
Two small clocks.
One piece of string,
Two precious rings.
That ought to do it,
Now comes the problem . . .
Biting into it!

Amy Wheeler
Woodville Primary School, South Woodham Ferrers

A Witch Sandwich

A witch sandwich is easy to make,
All you do is simply take . . .
A fluffy black rug,
A smashed purple mug,
Two dinosaur heads,
Ten butterflies' beds,
Six bat cakes
And nine rusty old rakes,
Five human lungs,
A spoonful of horse dung,
Four witches' hats
And nine black cats.
That ought to do it,
Now here comes the problem . . .
Biting into it!

Carly Newell (7)
Woodville Primary School, South Woodham Ferrers

A Witch Sandwich

A witch sandwich is easy to make
All you do is simply take . . .
A squashed toad
Found dead on the road
A cold cup of tea
And a stinging bumblebee
A big fat cat
That's eaten a rat
A slimy slug
And a crawling bug
That ought to do it
Now comes the problem . . .
Biting into it!

Luke Wiseman (7)
Woodville Primary School, South Woodham Ferrers

Witch

A witch sandwich is easy to make
All you do is simply take . . .
A spoonful of hay
A piece of clay
One huge gulp of mud
A slimy drink of blood
A horrible, muddy, old rug
A crawling bug I found in a rug
A lizard I found in a mug
That ought to do it
Now here comes the problem . . .
Biting into it.

Imogen Jones (8)
Woodville Primary School, South Woodham Ferrers

A Witch Sandwich

A witch sandwich is easy to make
All you do is simply take . . .
Two bat wings
Four diamond rings
Ten hissing snakes
One garden rake
Five singing cats
One smelly rat
A slice of bread
One human head
One child's hand
A grain of sand
That ought to do it
Now comes the problem . . .
Biting into it!

Libby Hargreaves (7)
Woodville Primary School, South Woodham Ferrers

Witch

A witch sandwich is easy to make
All you do is simply take . . .
One fat slimy frog,
That was sitting on a log.
Three wriggly worms,
That are covered in germs.
The wing of a bat,
The eye of a cat.
A lizard from a wizard
That was caught in a blizzard.
A bottle of blood
That's as thick as mud.
A speckly toad,
That was flat on the road.
A crocodile's rotten tooth
And a smelly old cow's hoof.
That ought to do it
Now here comes the problem . . .
Biting into it!

Connor Simpson (7)
Woodville Primary School, South Woodham Ferrers

A Wizard Sandwich

A wizard sandwich is easy to make
All you do is simply take . . .
A heap of dung,
A snake's tongue,
One ugly bat's head
And five frogs, all dead,
Two rotten eggs
And three human legs,
A rusty old rake
And a dead snake,
Five hundred live ants
And one pair of smelly pants,
A spoonful of blood
And five plant buds.
That ought to do it,
Now here comes the problem . . .
Biting into it!

William Martin (8)
Woodville Primary School, South Woodham Ferrers

Featured Author:

Maddie Stewart

Maddie is a children's writer, poet and author who currently lives in Coney Island, Northern Ireland.

Maddie has 5 published children's books, 'Cinders', 'Hal's Sleepover', 'Bertie Rooster', 'Peg' and 'Clever Daddy'. Maddie uses her own unpublished work to provide entertaining, interactive poems and rhyming stories for use in her workshops with children when she visits schools, libraries, arts centres and book festivals.

Favourites are 'Silly Billy, Auntie Millie' and 'I'm a Cool, Cool Kid'. Maddie works throughout Ireland from her home in County Down. She is also happy to work from a variety of bases in England. She has friends and family, with whom she regularly stays, in Leicester, Bedford, London and Ashford (Kent). Maddie's workshops are aimed at 5-11-year-olds. Check out Maddie's website for all her latest news and free poetry resources **www.maddiestewart.com**.

Read on to pick up some fab writing tips!

Nonsense Workshop

If you find silliness fun,
you will love nonsense poems.
Nonsense poems might describe silly things,
or people, or situations,
or, any combination of the three.

For example:

When I got out of bed today,
both my arms had run away.
I sent my feet to fetch them back.
When they came back, toe in hand
I realised what they had planned.
They'd made the breakfast I love most,
buttered spider's eggs on toast.

One way to find out if you enjoy nonsense poems is to start with familiar nursery rhymes. Ask your teacher to read them out, putting in the names of some children in your class.

Like this: Troy and Jill went up the hill
to fetch a pail of water.
Troy fell down
and broke his crown
and Jill came tumbling after.

If anyone is upset at the idea of using their name, then don't use it.

Did you find this fun?

Now try changing a nursery rhyme.
Keep the rhythm and the rhyme style, but invent a silly situation.

Like this: Hickory Dickory Dare
a pig flew up in the air.
The clouds above
gave him a shove
Hickory Dickory Dare.

Or this: Little Miss Mabel
sat at her table
eating a strawberry pie
but a big, hairy beast
stole her strawberry feast
and made poor little Mabel cry.

How does your rhyme sound if you put your own name in it?

Another idea for nonsense poems is to pretend letters are people and have them do silly things.

For example:

Mrs A	Mrs B	Mrs C
Lost her way	Dropped a pea	Ate a tree

To make your own 'Silly People Poem', think of a word to use.
To show you an example, I will choose the word 'silly'.
Write your word vertically down the left hand side of your page.
Then write down some words which rhyme with the sound of each letter.

S mess, dress, Bess, chess, cress
I eye, bye, sky, guy, pie, sky
L sell, bell, shell, tell, swell, well
L " " " " " " (" means the same as written above)
Y (the same words as those rhyming with I)

Use your rhyming word lists to help you make up your poem.

Mrs S made a mess
Mrs I ate a pie
Mrs L rang a bell
Mrs L broke a shell
Mrs Y said 'Bye-bye.'

You might even make a 'Silly Alphabet' by using all the letters of the alphabet.

It is hard to find rhyming words for all the letters. H, X and W are letters which are hard to match with rhyming words. I'll give you some I've thought of:

H - cage, stage, wage (close but not perfect)
X - flex, specs, complex, Middlesex
W - trouble you, chicken coop, bubble zoo

However, with nonsense poems, you can use nonsense words. You can make up your own words.

To start making up nonsense words you could try mixing dictionary words together. Let's make up some nonsense animals.

Make two lists of animals. (You can include birds and fish as well.)

Your lists can be as long as you like. These are lists I made:

elephant	kangaroo
tiger	penguin
lizard	octopus
monkey	chicken

Now use the start of an animal on one list and substitute it for the start of an animal from your other list.

I might use the start of oct/opus … oct and substitute it for the end of l/izard to give me a new nonsense animal … an octizard.
I might swap the start of monk/ey … monk with the end of kang/aroo To give me another new nonsense animal … a monkaroo.

What might a monkaroo look like? What might it eat?

You could try mixing some food words in the same way, to make up nonsense foods.

cabbage	potatoes
lettuce	parsley
bacon	crisps

Cribbage, bacley, and lettatoes are some nonsense foods made up from my lists.

Let's see if I can make a nonsense poem about my monkaroo.

My monkaroo loves bacley.
He'll eat lettatoes too
But his favourite food is cribbage
Especially if it's blue.

Would you like to try and make up your own nonsense poem?

Nonsense words don't have to be a combination of dictionary words. They can be completely 'made up'. You can use nonsense words to write nonsense sonnets, or list poems or any type of poem you like.

Here is a poem full of nonsense words:

I melly micked a turdle
and flecked a pendril's tum.
I plotineyed a shugat
and dracked a pipin's plum.

Ask your teacher to read it putting in some children's names instead of the first I, and he or she instead of the second I.

Did that sound funny?

You might think that nonsense poems are just silly and not for the serious poet. However poets tend to love language. Making up your own words is a natural part of enjoying words and sounds and how they fit together. Many poets love the freedom nonsense poems give them. Lots and lots of very famous poets have written nonsense poems. I'll name some: **Edward Lear**, **Roger McGough**, **Lewis Carroll**, **Jack Prelutsky** and **Nick Toczek**. Can you or your teacher think of any more? For help with a class nonsense poem or to find more nonsense nursery rhymes look on my website, **www.maddiestewart.com**. Have fun! Maddie Stewart.

Poetry Techniques

Here is a selection of poetry techniques with examples

Metaphors & Similes

A *metaphor* is when you describe your subject *as* something else, for example:
'Winter is a cruel master leaving the servants in a bleak wilderness'
whereas a *simile* describes your subject *like* something else i.e.
'His blue eyes are like ice-cold puddles' or 'The flames flickered like eyelashes'.

Personification

This is to simply give a personality to something that is not human, for example
'Fear spreads her uneasiness around' or 'Summer casts down her warm sunrays'.

Imagery

To use words to create mental pictures of what you are trying to convey,
your poem should awaken the senses and make the reader
feel like they are in that poetic scene ...
'The sky was streaked with pink and red as shadows
cast across the once-golden sand'.
'The sea gently lapped the shore as the palm trees rustled softly
in the evening breeze'.

Assonance & Alliteration

Alliteration uses a repeated constant sound and this effect can be quite striking:
'Smash, slippery snake slithered sideways'.
Assonance repeats a significant vowel or vowel sound to create an impact:
'The pool looked cool'.

Poetry Techniques

Repetition

By repeating a significant word the echo effect can be a very powerful way of enhancing an emotion or point your poem is putting across.

'The blows rained down, down,
Never ceasing,
Never caring
About the pain,
The pain'.

Onomatopoeia

This simply means you use words that sound like the noise you are describing, for example 'The rain *pattered* on the window' or 'The tin can *clattered* up the alley'.

Rhythm & Metre

The *rhythm* of a poem means 'the beat', the sense of movement you create. The placing of punctuation and the use of syllables affect the *rhythm* of the poem. If your intention is to have your poem read slowly, use double, triple or larger syllables and punctuate more often, where as if you want to have a fast-paced read use single syllables, less punctuation and shorter sentences. If you have a regular rhythm throughout your poem this is known as *metre*.

Enjambment

This means you don't use punctuation at the end of your line, you simply let the line flow on to the next one. It is commonly used and is a good word to drop into your homework!

Tone & Lyric

The poet s intention is expressed through their *tone*. You may feel happiness, anger, confusion, loathing or admiration for your poetic subject. Are you criticising or praising? How you feel about your topic will affect your choice of words and therefore your *tone*. For example 'I *loved* her', 'I *cared* for her', 'I *liked* her'. If you write the poem from a personal view or experience this is referred to as a *lyrical* poem. A good example of a lyrical poem is Seamus Heaney's 'Mid-term Break' or any sonnet!

YoungWriters

All About Shakespeare

Try this fun quiz with your family, friends or even in class!

1. Where was Shakespeare born?

....

2. Mercutio is a character in which Shakepeare play?

....

3. Which monarch was said to be 'quite a fan' of his work?

....

4. How old was he when he married?

....

5. What is the name of the last and 'only original' play he wrote?

....

6. What are the names of King Lear's three daughters?

....

7. Who is Anne Hathaway?

....

8. Which city is the play 'Othello' set in?

....

9. Can you name 2 of Shakespeare's 17 comedies?

....

10. 'This day is call'd the feast of Crispian: He that outlives this day, and comes safe home, Will stand a tip-toe when this day is nam'd, and rouse him at the name of Crispian' is a quote from which play?

....

11. Leonardo DiCaprio played Romeo in the modern day film version of Romeo and Juliet. Who played Juliet in the movie?

....

12. Three witches famously appear in which play?

....

13. Which famous Shakespearean character is Eric in the image to the left?

....

14. What was Shakespeare's favourite poetic form?

....

Answers are printed on the last page of the book, good luck!

If you would rather try the quiz online, you can do so at www.youngwriters.co.uk.

YoungWriters

Poetry Activity

Word Soup

To help you write a poem, or even a story, on any theme, you should create word soup!

If you have a theme or subject for your poem, base your word soup on it. If not, don't worry, the word soup will help you find a theme.

To start your word soup you need ingredients:

- Nouns (names of people, places, objects, feelings, i.e. Mum, Paris, house, anger)
- Colours
- Verbs ('doing words', i.e. kicking, laughing, running, falling, smiling)
- Adjectives (words that describe nouns, i.e. tall, hairy, hollow, smelly, angelic)

We suggest at least 5 of each from the above list, this will make sure your word soup has plenty of choice. Now, if you have already been given a theme or title for your poem, base your ingredients on this. If you have no idea what to write about, write down whatever you like, or ask a teacher or family member to give you a theme to write about.

Making Word Soup

Next, you'll need a sheet of paper.
Cut it into at least 20 pieces. Make sure the pieces are big enough to write your ingredients on, one ingredient on each piece of paper.
Write your ingredients on the pieces of paper.
Shuffle the pieces of paper and put them all in a box or bowl
- something you can pick the paper out of without looking at the words.
Pick out 5 words to start and use them to write your poem!

Example:

Our theme is winter. Our ingredients are:

- Nouns: snowflake, Santa, hat, Christmas, snowman.
- Colours: blue, white, green, orange, red.
- Verbs: ice-skating, playing, laughing, smiling, wrapping.
- Adjectives: cold, tall, fast, crunchy, sparkly.

**Our word soup gave us these 5 words:
snowman, red, cold, hat, fast and our poem goes like this:**

It's a *cold* winter's day,
My nose and cheeks are *red*
As I'm outside, building my *snowman*,
I add a *hat* and a carrot nose to finish,
I hope he doesn't melt too *fast*!

Tip: add more ingredients to your word soup and see how many different poems you can write!

Tip: if you're finding it hard to write a poem with the words you've picked, swap a word with another one!

Tip: try adding poem styles and techniques, such as assonance or haiku to your soup for an added challenge!

Young Writers Information

We hope you have enjoyed reading this book - and that you will continue to enjoy it in the coming years.

If you like reading and writing poetry drop us a line, or give us a call, and we'll send you a free information pack.

Alternatively, if you would like to order further copies of this book or any of our other titles, then please give us a call or log onto our website at www.youngwriters.co.uk.

Young Writers Information
Remus House
Coltsfoot Drive
Peterborough
PE2 9BF
Tel: (01733) 890066
Fax: (01733) 313524

Email: info@youngwriters.co.uk

Shakespeare Quiz Answers

1. Stratford-upon-Avon **2.** Romeo and Juliet **3.** James I **4.** 18 **5.** The Tempest **6.** Regan, Cordelia and Goneril **7.** His wife **8.** Venice **9.** All's Well That Ends Well, As You Like It, The Comedy of Errors, Cymbeline, Love's Labour's Lost, Measure for Measure, The Merchant of Venice, The Merry Wives of Windsor, A Midsummer Night's Dream, Much Ado About Nothing, Pericles - Prince of Tyre, The Taming of the Shrew, The Tempest, Twelfth Night, The Two Gentlemen of Verona, Troilus & Cressida, The Winter's Tale **10.** Henry V **11.** Claire Danes **12.** Macbeth **13.** Hamlet **14.** Sonnet